The Complete Guide to Baby Sign Language:

101 Tips and Tricks Every Parent Needs to Know

By Tracey Porpora

THE COMPLETE GUIDE TO BABY SIGN LANGUAGE: 101 TIPS AND TRICKS EVERY PARENT NEEDS TO KNOW

Library of Congress Cataloging-in-Publication Data

Porpora, Tracey, 1969-
  The complete guide to baby sign language : 101 tips and tricks every parent needs to know /
Tracey Porpora.
    p. cm.
  Includes bibliographical references and index.
  ISBN-13: 978-1-60138-393-8 (alk. paper)
  ISBN-10: 1-60138-393-2 (alk. paper)
  1. Nonverbal communication in infants. 2. Interpersonal communication in infants. 3.
Nonverbal communication in children. 4. Interpersonal communication in children. 5. Sign
language. 6. Language acquisition--Parent participation. I. Title.
  BF720.C65P67 2010
  419'.1--dc22
                              2009047058

PROJECT MANAGER: Kim Fulscher • PEER REVIEWER: Marilee Griffin
INTERIOR DESIGN: Holly Marie Gibbs • INTERIOR LAYOUT: Harrison Kuo
COVER DESIGN: Jackie Miller • millerjackiej@gmail.com

Printed in the United States

We recently lost our beloved pet "Bear," who was not only our best and dearest friend but also the "Vice President of Sunshine" here at Atlantic Publishing. He did not receive a salary but worked tirelessly 24 hours a day to please his parents. Bear was a rescue dog that turned around and showered myself, my wife, Sherri, his grandparents Jean, Bob, and Nancy, and every person and animal he met (maybe not rabbits) with friendship and love. He made a lot of people smile every day.

We wanted you to know that a portion of the profits of this book will be donated to The Humane Society of the United States. *–Douglas & Sherri Brown*

The human-animal bond is as old as human history. We cherish our animal companions for their unconditional affection and acceptance. We feel a thrill when we glimpse wild creatures in their natural habitat or in our own backyard.

Unfortunately, the human-animal bond has at times been weakened. Humans have exploited some animal species to the point of extinction.

The Humane Society of the United States makes a difference in the lives of animals here at home and worldwide. The HSUS is dedicated to creating a world where our relationship with animals is guided by compassion. We seek a truly humane society in which animals are respected for their intrinsic value, and where the human-animal bond is strong.

Want to help animals? We have plenty of suggestions. Adopt a pet from a local shelter, join The Humane Society and be a part of our work to help companion animals and wildlife. You will be funding our educational, legislative, investigative and outreach projects in the U.S. and across the globe.

Or perhaps you'd like to make a memorial donation in honor of a pet, friend or relative? You can through our Kindred Spirits program. And if you'd like to contribute in a more structured way, our Planned Giving Office has suggestions about estate planning, annuities, and even gifts of stock that avoid capital gains taxes.

Maybe you have land that you would like to preserve as a lasting habitat for wildlife. Our Wildlife Land Trust can help you. Perhaps the land you want to share is a backyard— that's enough. Our Urban Wildlife Sanctuary Program will show you how to create a habitat for your wild neighbors.

So you see, it's easy to help animals. And The HSUS is here to help.

THE HUMANE SOCIETY
OF THE UNITED STATES.

2100 L Street NW • Washington, DC 20037 • 202-452-1100
www.hsus.org

Dedication

To my mother, who told me I could, and to my daughter,
who showed me it was possible.

Table of Contents

Chapter 1: Why Use ASL to Communicate with a Hearing Baby?   25

Chapter 2: Gaining Perspective on ASL   35

Chapter 3: Get Started Now — Learn Sign Language for Yourself   47

Chapter 4: How and When Can I Begin to Teach My Infant Sign Language?   53

Chapter 5: Sign Language Teaching Tools   79

Chapter 6: How Can I Use Sign Language to Prevent Tantrums and to Potty Train?   89

Chapter 7: ASL Connected to Learning Skills 103

Chapter 8: Troubleshooting — Solving Common Sign Language Problems 115

Chapter 9: Should My Babysitter or Nanny Also Use Sign Language? 129

Chapter 10: Signing to Deaf and Hard-of-Hearing Children   137

Chapter 11: Becoming a Sign Language Professional   163

Chapter 12: Sign Language for Home and Public Schooling   181

Chapter 13: Parents' Point of View/Stories That Inspire   209

Foreword

I recall the first time I saw a baby sign to her mother. It was back when I attended graduate school at Penn State during the early 1980s as I was helping to conduct research about deaf parents' communication with their children. I watched deaf mothers effortlessly interact with their very young children. No tantrums were observed while parent and children spoke with their hands. At the time, I knew some sign language from my basic college sign language courses; however, nothing had prepared me for this observation. I witnessed no delays with discourse — simply communication between a mother and baby in its simplest form.

That is when I was sold on the idea that sign language could be instrumental with promoting language development for both deaf and hearing children. I know children can communicate much earlier and effectively when taught to sign by people who are their language models.

Leap ahead 25 years, and here I am writing the foreword to a wonderfully useful book about learning the basics of sign language with children: *The Complete Guide to Baby Sign Language: 101 Tips and Tricks Every Parent*

Needs to Know. In essence, Tracey Porpora and the book's contributors have set out to offer the readers a succinct explanation of the multitude of benefits of baby sign language combined with true-life experiences and helpful lessons to learn sign language. I was quite interested that Porpora provided essential background information about American Sign Language (ASL), which, in my opinion, should be the starting point in any true discussion about signing. The reader will learn how ASL has roots deeply imbedded within the deaf community. Yet, through the years, ASL has changed a bit to accommodate the communication needs of the hearing population wishing to learn this beautiful visual language. Thus, English and ASL have melded together in a way that provides communication between deaf and hearing. It also allows the hearing community to access this language to help promote or augment language with children and adults, including babies and individuals with special needs. In addition, I loved how Porpora paid respect toward the deaf culture, which is known for its rich history.

Advantages of sign language for babies and young children are clearly relayed in this book. I enjoyed reading the stories of the parents, educators, and researchers who shared their passion for sign language with young children. Early literacy with children is one of the many bonus outcomes for signing with young children. I truly enjoyed this chapter and feel that it is one of the compelling "arguments" as to why all schools should require basic sign language knowledge among their staff.

As a person who has dedicated her career to helping children with special needs, I was pleased to see Porpora include clear explanations as to the reasons children with learning, developmental, or even medical challenges could profit from using sign language. How wonderful for the families who have children with autism or Down syndrome to be able to establish a user-friendly mode of communication to augment other modalities, such as speech, picture exchange, or assistive technology. Also, children with medical speech impediments are also in need of being able to find an alternative form of communication to speech, which makes sign language the optimal choice.

I am always fascinated by how children so young can learn several languages within a short time frame as compared to adults. I always tell participants in my Signing Families workshops that, typically, developing children can usually learn more than one language at a time that is oral and visual. In my home, the children had been exposed as babies to three languages, including sign. The bilingual/trilingual aspect of this book, in my opinion, is very important, as so many of our children are raised in bilingual and bicultural homes today.

Parents and educators of all ages will be pleased to find a plethora of ideas sprinkled throughout the book to help adults learn about sign language and then act as role models for children to learn themselves. The ideas are easy and very manageable to include within a classroom, preschool, daycare, or home environments. Most important, they are fun, interactive, and engaging: all the ingredients to a good lesson.

Porpora has laid out an excellent resource and educational book for readers of *The Complete Guide to Baby Sign Language: 101 Tips and Tricks Every Parent Needs to Know*. It is a great way to start your sign language journey. Enjoy!

Sincerely,

Louise Masin Sattler, NCSP, M.S.
Founder and owner of Signing Families
www.signingfamilies.com

Introduction

Benefits of Teaching Your Baby Sign Language

One day, my daughter came home from preschool and started singing her graduation songs. Her words were accompanied by hand gestures, and I asked her if she was using sign language. She said yes, then showed me all the signs she had learned over the last year in school. There are no deaf children in her class, so I wondered why she was taught sign language. The answer to this question is simple: The school was teaching my child to be bilingual. Integrating some sign language into the curriculum is not any different from teaching children to count in Spanish or say "please" and "thank you" in French. You might be asking yourself, "Why do we need to talk with our hands?" It is obviously a benefit to people who are not verbal. Though that includes deaf individuals, it also applies to understanding babies who are not yet able to talk but are perfectly capable of knowing when they want something, are hungry, or have wet diapers. A baby who is 6 months old has the developmental ability to communicate with his parents, yet he does not yet have the verbal skills to do so. A baby at 6 months has developed the muscles in her hands needed to perform signs and has the ability to understand the basic elements of what people are saying to her. However, the baby's vocal cords have not developed enough to utter the words necessary for you to understand her. But a baby will often flail her arms when she is happy and know to point to an object she wants you to give her. She can wave "bye-bye," and likes to grab your finger and squeeze it as tight as she possibly can. Because she has the ability to use her hands to tell you what she wants, as well as the developmental capability to know what she wants, babies can learn to use sign language to communicate.

Sign Language for Babies

Armed with this visual language, your child can tell you exactly what he wants and when he wants it. Teaching your baby sign language also helps him avoid the frustration that often occurs in infants and toddlers who simply cannot verbalize what they are feeling. Another benefit of teaching your child sign language is it allows you to bond earlier with your preverbal baby. It allows you to share the earliest communications he can express with you. For example, Lora Heller, founder of Baby Fingers LLC (which offers sign language classes for parents and children in New York City) said her son's first sign was "I love you" at just 6 months old. Imagine your tiny baby having the ability and tools to tell you he loves you.

Long-Term Benefits of Baby Sign Language

While many parents use signing to communicate with their children, they often stop doing so once the baby can verbalize what she wants or needs. The reason for this is because the baby no longer needs to sign, as she can verbally tell you what she wants. However, there are a growing number of parents who recognize the benefits of teaching their children sign language as they learn more words. This way, you are creating a bilingual child and giving your baby another form of communication that can enhance her learning abilities.

Several studies conducted by leaders in the sign language field revealed that children who learn sign language as infants have the potential to talk and read earlier. Just ask Dr. Linda Acredolo and Dr. Susan Goodwyn, who were among the first to discover the relationship between preverbal babies and sign language. In 1996, they wrote their first book detailing how to teach babies sign language. The pair developed "Baby Sign" classes, a program that certifies budding sign language professionals to teach baby sign language that is loosely based on ASL.

Their study findings revealed that infants who were taught sign language spoke earlier, achieved higher IQ scores, and used more words than their non-signing counterparts. Their research was spurred in 1982 when Acredolo's 1-year-old daughter was caught performing the hand gestures that commonly accompany the song "The Itsy-Bitsy Spider." On another occasion, she performed a gesture of sniffing an imaginary flower when she spotted one in a garden.

These early gestures were the catalyst for Acredolo and Goodwyn's research, which included a study between babies who knew signals and those who did not. More than 140 families with babies who were just 11 months old participated in the study. Each child was tested using "standardized language measures" at the following milestone ages: 11, 15, 19, 24, 30, and 36 months old. The findings revealed that babies who were exposed to and eventually used symbolic gestures, such as signing, learned to speak more easily — and, in many cases, faster, than those preverbal babies who were not introduced to this form of communication. Babies who were 2 years old had mastered vocabulary equivalent to that of a 27- or 28-month-old, which is a three-month advanced stage. The study also found that 3-year-old baby signers spoke more like 47-month-olds, which amounts to an 11-month advancement. Many of these children were retested at age 8; those who had signed scored an average of 12 points higher on the Wechsler Intelligence Scale for Children, third edition test (WISC-III) than those children who were not taught sign language. The WISC-III test, developed in 1991, is used to measure children's intelligence. Though the test does not require reading or writing, it is administered to children verbally as a set of subtests. A normal IQ score ranges between 90 and 109, whereas scores over 120 are considered high.

Help for Speech-Delayed Children

Parents with speech-delayed children often experience an overwhelming amount of frustration watching their child try to communicate with them without words. For this reason, many speech pathologists use sign language to help communicate with speech- delayed children, as well as special-needs children who can not yet use their verbal skills. Imagine how less frustrated a verbally challenged 3-year-old will be when he cannot talk, but can still tell you what he wants through this visual language.

Did You Know?

"You can start teaching sign language as soon as a baby is born. Your baby may not perform a sign right away, but she is absolutely learning from infancy."

— Heather M. Kendel, founder and executive director of ASL Advocates

What is American Sign Language?

American Sign Language (ASL) has its own linguistics, grammar, and sentence structure that is different from any other language. Sign language it not universal; it is unique to its own country, so ASL is different from British or French Sign Language. The foundation of sign language dates back to the 1770s in France where a priest named Abbé Charles-Michel de l'Épée established the first school for deaf people in Paris. In the early 1800s, Thomas Hopkins Gallaudet, a minister from New England, met

Laurent Clerc, a deaf individual who knew sign language, and together they brought sign language to the United States by establishing the American Asylum in Hartford, Connecticut, in 1817.

However, most advocates of baby sign language will admit that although they use ASL signs or finger-spelled words to teach babies sign language, they do it in English grammar structure. ASL is its own language with its own grammar and sentence structure. In ASL, there is an order of how signs are produced: If you want to say, "I want to go to the store tomorrow," you would sign, "Tomorrow store go I."

Is Sign Language Easy to Learn?

You may wonder how you will ever be able to master a second, visual language, when you are learning so many things for the first time as a new parent. However, by taking some time now to learn a few simple signs — such as "more," "milk," "wet," and "all done" — you may make your life a lot easier a few months down the road. It will come in handy when your child knows he needs a diaper change and can sign these words to you before he can say them. You will have saved yourself some intense moments trying to figure out why your baby will not stop crying at 2 a.m.

Although it is a visual language, ASL allows you to convey feelings. What many people do not know is that ASL offers many opportunities to express emotions through eye contact, body language, and other gestures that can accompany your hand signs. ASL can be performed in two ways:

- "Fingerspelling," or using the signs for each letter in a word you want to say.

- Using the sign for each word in the English language.

Can I Really Teach an Infant Sign Language?

You may be thinking, "I barely know how to change a diaper, and you want me to learn to teach my baby a whole new language?" But babies learn sign language much like they learn any other language: by watching you sign over and over again. So if you say "Mama" over and over, your baby ultimately says those words; it is the same with signing. If you keep making the sign for "Mommy," which is two fingers tapping on your chin while saying the word, your baby will eventually mimic that gesture. Hence, she has made her first sign.

What You Will Learn From This Book

From using props, such as a red ball when you sign "red" or "ball," to signing the words in your baby's favorite song, there are many proven techniques that will help you teach sign language to your preverbal infant. And the benefits are plentiful. This book is your complete resource for learning to teach your baby sign language. Together with your baby, you will travel this path to learning ASL together. This book will tell you when and where signing is most valuable to your infant, and how to pick the signs that will allow your child to best express his early needs to you. You will learn how to integrate signing into your current non-signing household, and how to get other family members, nannies, and babysitters on board with your signing goals. Set realistic goals: Your baby is not likely going to sign before he is 6 months old. In fact, most children will not sign before they are 1 year old. Some parents will attest that it took a whole year of integrating sign language into their daily routine before their baby even remotely attempted to sign.

But once you have learned some signs and teach them to your baby, this book will show you how they can be used to build self-esteem and how to teach your baby to sign what he wants before he can get upset.

By the time you are finished this book, you will be able to:

- Communicate with your preverbal baby through sign language.

- Have sign language help end the frustration of your preverbal baby's inability to communicate with you.

- Use the best tips to teach and reinforce each sign.

- Troubleshoot any problems, such as your baby's reluctance to sign back.

- Use sign language to help your speech-delayed or special-needs child better communicate with you.

- Know when it is appropriate to use sign language in your every-day life.

- Learn how to use sign language to potty train your child.

- Learn how to pick and choose the best sign language classes for you and your baby.

- Teach your deaf child sign language.

- Pursue a career that utilizes your ASL skills.

- Use sign language in an elementary school classroom.

And if you get the hang of this all relatively quickly, you may want to continue using sign language once your child begins to speak. You may want to see how far you can go to enhance his development with the use of sign language.

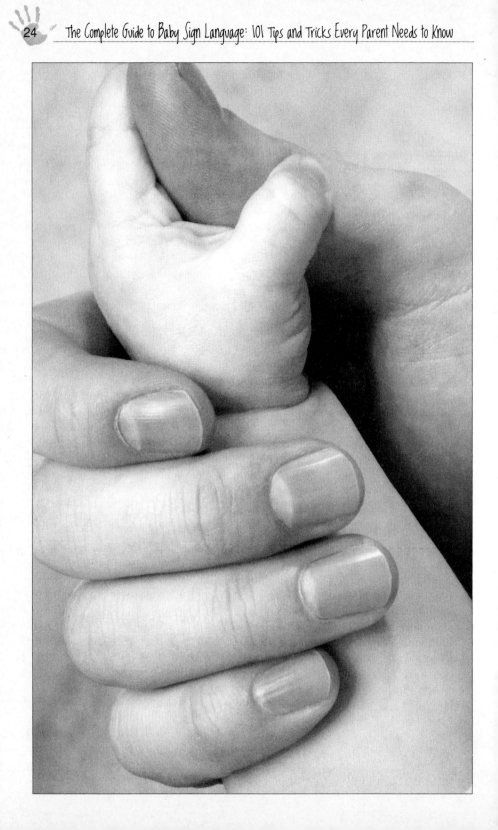

Chapter One

Why Use ASL to Communicate with a Hearing Baby?

F rom that first moment in the delivery room when your baby started to cry, she was telling you something. If she could talk, she may be saying: "What just happened? Where am I? What is this place? And who are you?" Soon after this traumatic transition from the womb to the world, your baby is learning. At a very young age, she begins to recognize that you are her parent.

From birth, your baby begins the learning process. From the time her little eyes can focus on you, she is studying you to learn what she needs to grow, thrive, and survive in this world. Babies have the innate ability from birth to begin to process information they can see. In other words, they visually begin the learning process. Although a baby who has been watching you for the last six months knows she wants milk or needs a diaper change, she cannot say it to you. All she can do is cry, coo, or use facial expressions, such as frowns, lip puckers, and smiles. But if you give this baby of yours a means of communication, then she can tell you through sign language that she is wet, that she needs more of something, or that the color red simply makes her happy. Be aware that as you embark on this route to teaching your baby sign language, you will likely encounter someone who will tell you this will not work. However, the naysayer is often amazed — and sometimes perplexed — that your baby has been able to communicate with you before she could speak. Through sign language, your baby will begin to talk to you about her world and the things that are important to her.

Did You Know?

"Babies will learn through association. Every time they see the sign for milk, they will know it is milk. They begin to understand this gesture means this."

— Barbara Desmarais, a Canada-based parenting and life coach who teaches sign language to babies

CASE STUDY: LORA HELLER

Lora Heller, Founder of Baby Fingers LLC
Author of several sign language books
for babies and adults
Music therapist/Teacher of the deaf
585 West End Ave. #12E
New York, NY 10024 | 212-874-5978
lora@mybabyfingers.com

Lora Heller's interest in ASL was sparked when she was a camp counselor at age 16. That year, she met an 11-year-old deaf camper, and with him she learned to sign. In 2000, Heller developed Baby Fingers LLC, which offers creative sign language classes for grown-ups and children together, newborn through age 3, and some classes for older children and adults.

It is our goal at Baby Fingers to provide families with an opportunity for bonding, communication, and a jump-start in language development through sign language and the arts. Through the focus on language, parents are spending more time with their children, helping to strengthen the bond and demonstrate the significance of the relationship. There is a greater amount of communication and a focus on being together.

At Baby Fingers, we use songs, stories, and games to engage the children and provide parents with a memory aid so they can utilize the signs at home right away. We offer a lot of repetition and explanation of how to incorporate the signs into their routines at home. We begin every class with a "hello" song and end with a "goodbye" song. We sing songs such as The "More We Get Together" to teach the signs for "more" and "friends," and we read stories such as "Brown Bear, Brown Bear, What Do You See?" to teach signs for animals and colors.

My children were able to communicate using a true language to ask for "more," "milk," a "diaper change," "music," to tell me that Daddy took the train, and to express emotions. They were both early talkers, and when I could not understand them, the signs helped to clarify their speech. We still sign together. Sign language provides a means for communication with an actual language. I believe children learn about the importance of family and the ability to express themselves through language.

Foster Language Skills

Once your baby is signing, she is now eager to mimic Mom and Dad once again and will start saying the words that she hears her parents say when she makes a sign. So she may make a "ba ba" sound, and with it make the sign for ball. Because your baby is armed with this visual language, you know that your baby is trying to say ball — and not bottle — and you can work on reinforcing the sign, as well as her early verbal skills. In this instance, sign language has aided in helping your child learn new words and what these words mean.

Remember: Your baby wants to communicate with you; she wishes she could say the words to do so, but she cannot. If you introduce sign language to her, she will likely be eager to make the signs with her tiny hands and communicate back to you what she is feeling, thinking, or really wants. When you use sign language to accompany your spoken words, you tend to be deliberate with pronunciation, and you also tend to be repetitive with your speech. While feeding your baby cereal, you might ask her "Do you want more?" with an emphasis on the word "more." Because your baby will hear you clearly pronounce this word over and over in the sign language learning stage, then when she is ready to speak, this will likely be one of her first words.

Sign language will help you work with your child on her early speaking skills, and you will be more focused on the words she is trying to say and helping her pronounce them correctly. Because of this, her early vocabulary words will come easier if you, as her parent, know what she is trying to say through sign language.

Children who learn sign language as babies will also experience an increased vocabulary. Non-speech delayed children who are taught sign language from infancy will have a vocabulary of about 50 words that includes two-word phrases, such as "get up" or "go bye-bye" by the age of 2.

When a baby is 18 months old, she typically has a vocabulary of five to 20 words. By 2 years old, that vocabulary often grows between 150 to 300 words. Baby signers of at least 2 years old have been reported to say 50 more words than their non-signing friends. The reason for this is that if a child is exposed to sign language at a young age, she is connecting the signs with the spoken words. If she has mastered 50 signs she can make with her hands, then once her vocal cords allow her to speak, she will want to master the spoken words to match her sign language vocabulary.

Increase Communication Skills

If you start signing with your child at a young age, you will allow yourself and your baby to have a different family dynamic than that found in a non-signing household. Research has shown that children as young as 6 to 8 months old can begin to mimic gestures they are shown. In the 1970s, Dr. Joseph Garcia wrote his master's thesis while attending the University of Alaska, which focused on how preverbal babies could communicate with their parents via sign language. In his research, he revealed that hearing babies could use sign language as early as 6 months old. In his later research included in the book, Garcia said children who knew sign language as part of their early language had an "above-average understanding of English syntax earlier" than non-signing peers. The non-signing children in his study were only beginning to identify items in their world with verbal vocabulary, while their signing counterparts were already speaking about the same objects. He also uncovered that once these signing babies found their words to speak, they often had a better command and grasp of the English language than those children who never signed.

However, it is important to note that the rate at which your child begins to sign is individual. All children will learn at their own pace, as they do for all other milestones in their lives, such as crawling, talking, and walking. And it is common for a parent to sign to their babies for six months to a year before the baby signs back. Giving your child this early means of communication leads to a less frustrated, more satisfied child because she is able to communicate with you from the beginning.

As your baby enters toddlerhood and has mastered a few signs, she may be able to add emotion to them as well, but how can you convey emotion without words? Because ASL is a visual language, it gives you the opportunity to express yourself physically. If you show intensity with signs by using facial expressions, eye contact, and body language, your child may add intensifiers to let you know she is "really" tired or "very" hungry.

Also important to convey emotion in signing is eye contact. When using sign language, it is imperative to make eye contact with the person you are signing to, and this includes your preverbal baby. You need to look into your child's eyes, say the word for the sign, and make the sign. She needs to see the expression on your face, the pronunciation of the words, and the visual sign. When you look into her eyes, you can see that she is watching you and making these visual connections.

Stimulate Cognitive Skills

If you are a parent, you have probably heard the term "cognitive skills." But you may have been reluctant or embarrassed to ask exactly what these highly touted skills are. Cognitive skills are needed for your baby to process information, objects, sight, and sound. It is simply the way your baby develops her perception of the world around her. By signing with your preverbal baby, you are developing her brain power. Your baby is making the connection between the sign you are making with your hands and the words you are speaking. In fact, you are laying the groundwork for her foundation of learning. You are stimulating her brain to visually think. In addition, you are making an impact on her learning skills that she will rely on in the future. Your baby will begin to use her hands to communicate with you, and this is a means of stimulating her early cognitive skills. When you sign, make the sign as close to your face as you can. This will allow your baby to see the sounds come out of your mouth for the word, and at the same time she will see the sign.

Develop Fine Motor Skills

What better way to exercise the small muscles in your baby's hands than have her learn sign language? As we grow, our muscles are forming, and learning sign language helps your baby learn — and eventually master — fine motor skills. Fine motors skills develop as your baby learns to tug at your hair or pull a puppy's tail in a playful gesture. Those actions are the first signs your baby's fine motor skills are developing. Signing can only enhance her dexterity and promote fine motor skill growth. However, you need to remember your baby is developing her fine motor skills as you teach sign language; hence, her first sign may not be perfect. But that is all right. This is commonly referred to as "sign approximation," whereby your baby will make the sign to the best of her ability using her developing fine motor skills. For example, you have taught your daughter the sign for "eat," which is holding all your fingers up to your mouth in a gesture that appears as if you were going to put food in your mouth. But maybe she will just put her thumb near her mouth when she wants to make the sign for eat. This would be her approximation of the sign. This is your daughter's way of making the sign. Is it wrong? As long as you, the parent or caregiver, understand that this is her version of the sign for eat, it is fine. You should continue to model the sign properly when you say the word, and as she continues to better develop fine motor skills, she will likely master the sign correctly in time.

It is important to note that ASL signs can be divided into two major groups:

- **Image-based signs:** These signs appear to mimic an image of the word you are saying. For example, the sign for phone is your hand next to your ear, with your thumb closest to your ear and pinky finger near your mouth. Hence, the sign is based on the image of you talking on the telephone.

- **Abstract signs:** These signs may be more difficult for your child to learn, as they have no correlation to the spoken word. For example, tapping your chin with two fingers makes the word "Mom." This has nothing to do with the image of mother (unless it is Mom who is making the sign, of course), but those are signs you and your child will more likely need to remember simply by memory.

Form an Early Bond

We all bond with our babies in many different ways. From breastfeeding and giving baths, to reading bedtime stories and playing games, we initiate and form that parental connection with our little one in various ways from the time she is born. Sign language is yet another bonding tool for you to grow closer to your baby. If she can effectively tell you what she wants and you can attend to her needs because of this, then the bond between you grows stronger.

Sign language also gives you something else to do with your baby. Instead of simply laying her on a mat or in a playpen, sign language forces you to make eye contact with your baby. You are now forced to do something physical that requires you to be in her view.

It is important to note that there are several different forms of sign language in the United States. In addition to ASL, other currently used forms of sign language include:

- **Signed English:** Signing the words as you speak them in the English language structure, rather than using the ASL syntax, is signed English. Signed English is most likely what you will use with your preverbal baby to communicate.

- **Signing Exact English (SEE):** Using sign language in English grammar structure as part of a system of manual communication is SEE. Devised in 1972, it utilizes many signs from ASL but also uses modified handshapes. It often uses the shapes of a letter rather than the ASL sign for the letter. SEE is often thought of as a code for visually representing words spoken in English.

However, it is important to note that ASL is the only form of sign language used in the country that is a true language.

Did You Know?

"Your baby wants to make conversation with you. She may look out the window and see a bird, but it is totally invisible to you right now because you are a new parent and you are sleep-deprived. You are focusing on getting your baby to eat her meal. But your baby signs the word 'bird.' Your baby does not want the bird or need the bird; she just wanted in on the conversation."

— Dawn Babb Prochovnic, founder of SmallTalk Learning

CASE STUDY: BETH BLAIR

Parent from Oro Valley, Arizona
(520) 219-3349
bethblairwrites@gmail.com

Beth Blair began signing with her son Jeb, who is now 5 years old, when he was 8 months old. He began signing back by the age of 10 months. Blair attended a baby sign language class and learned a few basic signs. After that, she went online and began memorizing the signs most relevant to her son's world. That list eventually expanded to more than 50 signs.

My son cried regularly until he could crawl at 6 months of age. Though being able to get around on his own helped, he would still easily become extremely frustrated. I began practicing sign language and found he would respond to my signs before he could sign back. It was as if the signs were "louder" than verbal communication in a way. Instead of being frustrated and blocking out my verbal words, he could see and understand the signs. By 10 months old, he was signing. Life changed from that moment on.

His first signs were made only days apart. Jeb started out with the basics: "milk," "eat," and "diaper change." He expanded to items, such as airplanes and animals, including a "cat," "dog," "cow," "horse," "duck," and "bird." One of the signs he used most frequently was "help." Using that one sign made more of a difference than anything. If he could not get a toy to work or he dropped something out of reach, he learned all he had to do was ask.

My son was able to carry on as if he were a speaking child. As he grew, he continued to learn more and more signs. Other parents were stunned at his abilities. But I truly believe anyone can teach their child sign language — it simply takes patience and perseverance.

I found signing connected us. We could be at a playgroup in complete chaos, and he would look at me from across the room and tell me he needed a diaper change or water. The overall benefit of learning sign language for our family was that my son's frustration dissipated. He now had a way of expressing himself to my husband and me, and that was priceless. I believe signing helped his cognitive abilities. His teachers are always amazed that since age 2 he could focus on one task, such as art projects or building towers, and he always sees it through to the end.

My son is a June baby and has always been the youngest in his preschool class, yet he was the first potty-trained child in his class of 2 year olds. I think signing "diaper change" made him aware of his body, and being able to communicate that need certainly helped him to become potty trained earlier.

I found persistence to be the key in building this communication breakthrough. I urge other parents to try, and not to feel bad if the baby does not respond to signing. My daughter only used one sign, "milk," for about two months, then began speaking. Every child is different, and it is important to celebrate that. I am thankful I had the opportunity to expose my son to a unique way of communicating.

Did You Know?

"It takes a long time to teach your children to talk. Everything they hear takes them a long time to understand, and be able to form the verbal sounds with their mouths. Most babies start with 'ma ma' and 'da da' because those are the easiest things to say."

— Heather M. Kendel, founder and executive director of ASL Advocates

Chapter Two

Gaining Perspective on ASL

A Psychological Perspective on Baby Sign Language

While teaching your hearing baby sign language is a relatively new concept to the 21st-century parent, it has also gained mixed reviews from the medical community at large. Though some psychologists and medical professionals tout the idea of teaching hearing babies sign language, there is a small group of critics who claim children can become lax in their speaking abilities if they have begun to rely heavily on sign language. In this instance, the child has grown so used to signing, he does not see the need to speak.

More general criticism of baby sign language that has been reported in media points out that the use of too many signs can overburden and overwhelm a child in his early stages of life. Critics in the medical field say parents can bombard children with too many signs, causing the child to feel overwhelmed at such an early stage in his life. However, many professionals in the sign language and speech pathology community negate critics' belief that baby sign language can inhibit speech, and say that signing — as much or as little as a parent chooses to do it — instead makes a baby eager to learn the word to match the sign he already knows.

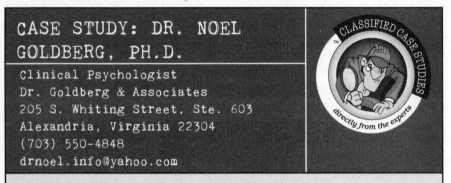

CASE STUDY: DR. NOEL GOLDBERG, PH.D.

Clinical Psychologist
Dr. Goldberg & Associates
205 S. Whiting Street, Ste. 603
Alexandria, Virginia 22304
(703) 550-4848
drnoel.info@yahoo.com

Dr. Noel Goldberg is a clinical psychologist who obtained her doctorate in clinical psychology (Psy.D.) from the Virginia Consortium. Prior to this degree, she earned a master's degree in educational psychology from University of North Carolina at Chapel Hill. She believes sign language is beneficial to babies, and gives advice on what to do if you think sign language is hindering the child's verbal skills.

Developmentally, because young children do not have the ability to speak, sign language gives them a voice. As an added benefit, they are learning another language, which could be a primer to learning more languages later.

However, sign language may hinder communication if the child chooses not to use words when he is able. At this point, the parent may want to seek out professional help (such as speech therapists or developmental psychologists). But the parent can also stop using sign language and help their child shift to using words. With the verbal world, communicating with words and voices is strongly reinforced, so I do not expect children will remain using a language that is not fully applicable to more people. Imagine taking a child to a candy store, and the clerk asking the child what he wants: Eventually, he will have to "say" and speak. Children also have to get accustomed to sounds, voices, and vocabulary. As parents, you can spend time teaching your children to read. I think sign language helps children learn interaction styles and again, gives them a sense of agency. They soon realize that their actions (signs) lead to responses, and they want to learn more ways to utilize signs.

By teaching babies to communicate at an early age, you are giving them the initial tools they will need for the lifelong task of communicating. I believe that by getting them to use their brain and hands early on, you are strengthening these "muscles" and probably improving hand-eye coordination, and the ability to think and learn cause-effect relationships.

Think of a child who is disabled and can only use a computer with a pointer. This becomes the manner in which he can communicate. Think of sign language as a tool, and the consumer has to learn how to use the tool.

Sign language can also help a child learn ways to communicate without using his voice, and may foster an ability to pay attention to others (those who are communicating). This will, in the future, help socialization and possibly schooling

because a child is conditioned to look at someone to read the language and therefore will be paying attention to him. If learning sign language and using it makes children enjoy communicating, then they may want to learn other languages. Sign language is the precursor to communicating with words and voice expression and can assist babies with learning the social cues involved when they interact with one another.

I think if parents are frustrated with how they interact with their child because their baby has trouble communicating with words, sign language may be helpful. Sign language helps "brain muscles" because it causes children to think, remember signs, and learn cause-effect relationships. By signing, the child has a sense of agency and realizes he can act on his environment (assuming the parent is responsive to the signs). Is this not what communication is all about, either giving information or having others respond?

Setting the Stage for a Bilingual or Trilingual Child

Sign language, while not oral, is still a language. When you teach your child ASL, you are exposing him to another language. Hence, you are teaching him to be bilingual. However, if you decide to teach your child some basic signs before he can talk, and when he becomes a 2-year-old chatterbox you drop the signing, your child is not going to become bilingual with sign language as his second language. But if you continue to use sign language in your household as your child speaks and discovers new words, then you will be exposing him to this language. It is likely that in his preschool daycare center, sign language will be used in some fashion. There also is the option of enrolling your child in sign language classes. But most importantly, you also can continue to teach your child ASL, even if you are learning alongside him.

Once your child is comfortable using this visual language along with his spoken words, sign language can be the bridge to learning yet a third or fourth language. For example, if you are fluent in Spanish and want to begin to teach your child some Spanish words, you can use sign language to help him understand the meaning of the words. If you desire to teach your child the Spanish word for house, say "casa," and make the ASL sign for "house."

Because your child recognizes this visual sign, he now relates the Spanish word with the sign as well as the English word. In this instance, sign language is a visual aid to learning a third language. If your child is offered Spanish, French, or Mandarin in school, use sign language with him at home while he practices homework. This will reinforce his learning of the other languages and will help groom a trilingual child. If your child is not completely fluent in sign language, it is all right. He can also learn more sign language along with the third language, which makes learning fun and visual at the same time. As he learns the Spanish word for car, "coche," he can also learn the sign for "car" at this time. Now he will relate the new sign to the new word, and you can say and sign the word "car" in English and Spanish before you get into your car each day.

CASE STUDY: DR. DOLORES M. SWITAJ, PH.D.

Psychologist and Supervisor of Infant Toddler Program
PSE&G Children's Specialized Hospital
200 Somerset Street
New Brunswick, New Jersey 08901
(732) 258-7085
dswitaj@childrens-specialized.org

Dr. Dolores M. Switaj has more than 20 years of experience in psychology, working in clinics, schools, and hospitals. She has worked primarily with children under 5 and with children diagnosed with a diverse array of medical issues. She has worked several years in neonatal intensive care unit (NICU) settings and rehab programs. She has been trained in administering early childhood developmental measures. Switaj believes children are developmentally able to communicate with signs much earlier than they can speak. She says signing is a tool that allows even very small children to express themselves.

When signs are taught in conjunction with spoken words, the benefits include stimulation of intellectual development, enhanced self-esteem, strengthened parent/infant bonding, accelerated speech processes, and expanded social opportunities for communication.

If you start using signs with your child, he will reciprocate when he is ready, depending on the age of your child, or if the child has physical, mental, or developmental delays.

According to Lev Vygotsky, a psychologist and social constructivist, social interaction plays an important role in language acquisition. Sign language is based on social interaction. Signs can be taught to babies within the first year of life. Dr. Joseph Garcia indicated in his research that babies who are exposed to sign regularly and consistently at 6 to 7 months of age could begin using signs effectively by 8 to 9 months of age. The underlying idea is that babies are capable of coordinating their motor system (hands, arms, fingers) earlier than they can coordinate their vocal system (lips, tongue, diaphragm). The earlier any child is exposed to and begins to acquire language, the better that child's communication skills will eventually become.

ASL is a second language. Research has shown that being multilingual expands cognitive processes and intellectual skills. It boosts lingual development and often promotes the ability to learn additional languages.

Teaching a child gestures (signs) paired along with spoken words actually encourages earlier communication. Once the child catches on to the process, she is more quickly able to understand and communicate with the world around her. The child can initiate communication exchanges instead of being a passive observer. The child learns to communicate needs, and the parent is better able to meet those needs. Facial expressions clarifies the emotion of the communicator in spoken language, and through sign language, children begin to learn the effect associated with social interactions.

Gestures are a natural means of communication used all over the world. Professionals who have introduced sign language to young children find that it does not hinder communication or the development of verbal skills. In fact, researchers report that babies who sign learn to speak months earlier than average. If the goal is communication, then signing will meet that communication need much earlier than speech. Because speaking remains a goal, words are usually

The Use of Sign Language with Special-Needs and Speech-Delayed Children

Children usually begin to speak between 10 and 18 months of age. Usually, a child's first words are "ma ma" and "da da." The signing baby will often speak the words he knows how to sign in his early vocabulary. But children who are speech delayed may not speak one word until they are age 2 or older. In many cases, these children have become extremely frustrated because they cannot communicate with you the way their peers are communicating, and this may result in tantrums and unfavorable behavior. However, sign language can ignite verbal communication for a speech-delayed child because once the frustration of not being able to communicate is gone, the verbal ability comes more easily. While many children are simply speech delayed, others may be unable to formulate their words due to a developmental disorder, such as autism or Down syndrome. Many parents, such as Lesa J. Thayer of Fruita, Colorado, say sign language has greatly bridged the gap between an autistic child and the parents from a young age.

CASE STUDY: LESA J. THAYER

Parent from Fruita, Colorado
lt63@bresnan.bet

Because her husband's sister had a hearing disability, Lesa J. Thayer learned some sign language from her family members. Later, she learned her son was autistic. Because he was not talking, his speech therapist began using sign language with him. She believes this was the beginning of bridging her communication gap with her son, who is now 26 years old.

I started signing with easy, useful signs, such as "milk," "apple," "no," "yes," "stop," "puppy," "sit," "I love you," "boy," and "girl." We began signing when my son, Adam, was about 1 year old. Adam learned to sign before talking. It helped him pair the sign with the visual word with the use of his mouth to start talking.

He made his first sign immediately. He started learning the signs for "puppy," "sit," "stop," "yes," and "no." It made it easier for him to tell me what he wanted. He would not have had the advantage of communication at the age he did, and this would have created a further delay. We could talk across a room or store as he became mobile.

He was able to tell me what he wanted but also was able to understand things visually versus just auditory. He is still very visual. Pairing words and visual aids make learning so much easier and effective for him. Signing gave him an advantage in learning. Adam also learned to read using the visual assistance of sign.

The doctors told me he would never walk, talk, ride a bike, or read. Signing gave him the edge toward enhancing his learning to read, talk, and use language.

Adam had quicker progress then expected, and I think that was due to sign language. He grew up to function well and live alone while maintaining independence. I am so proud of him.

Natural language progression is not taking place when there is no conversation between you and your child. You find yourself asking questions and trying to guess what your child's answer is. Often, if your child is speech delayed, you will seek the help of a speech language pathologist or therapist, who can help with speaking issues.

A speech language pathologist will engage your child through focused language stimulation. For example, if you take a stuffed bear, you can show the child the signs for "bear." Next, you may want to color a picture of a bear, and again make the sign. Later, you can read the story "The Three Little Bears," so you essentially bombard the child with the signs and the word, giving her every opportunity to make the connection between the sign and the word for bear.

To help your speech-delayed child, the speech language pathologist often will make the sign for your child "hand over hand," meaning he or she will take your son's hands and help him make the sign until he can make the sign on his own. Speech language pathologists will often use focused stimulation with several signs at a time. Your child may enter a play area where there will be a train set. The speech language pathologist will model the signs for car, train, track and house, while your child plays with the train. The speech language pathologist will then make your child do the sign, and all the while he or she will be saying the words attached to the signs.

You can continue this type of learning with your child at home. Put your child in a playful situation where you can sign relevant words and model those signs for her.

```
CASE STUDY: DR. SUSAN
HENDLER LEDERER, PH.D.
Adelphi University
Department of Communication Sciences
& Disorders
Hy Weinberg Center
158 Cambridge Avenue
Garden City, New York 11530
lederer@adelphi.edu
```

Dr. Susan Hendler Lederer, a certified speech-language pathologist since 1981, is an associate professor in communication sciences and disorders at Adelphi University since 1997. She obtained her Ph.D. in speech-language pathology from New York University in 1996.

When I arrived at Adelphi University in 1997, I initiated "grown-up and me"-style language enrichment groups, called TOTalk, to help toddlers learn to communicate. Since the inception of TOTalk, we have introduced signs along with first words to hundreds of young children. Research on the efficacy of these groups has been published in peer-reviewed journals and presented nationally.

Working with these children inspired me to write two children's books, *I Can Say That* (Children's Publishing, 2006) and *I Can Do That* (Children's Publishing, 2008), designed to encourage first words. In both books, signs and/or natural gestures are provided for each targeted vocabulary word.

I work with our clinical supervisors to create curricular activities and treatment protocols that are research-based. My area of research expertise is selecting and facilitating first words. We use a proven language facilitation technique called focused stimulation. Basically, we provide the child with multiple models of the target vocabulary with its sign. We help the child sign with hand-over-hand. If the child does not imitate the sign or word right away, we do not persist. Research has shown the multiple exposures are what is really important. The child's production will follow.

In addition to the research on children developing normally, researchers studying children with language delays have also reported on the efficacy of using signs in conjunction with words. Speech is the finest fine motor act in the body. Many children with language delays also have speech delays. Parents should not be concerned that using signs will slow the use of speech; research proves this is not the case. In fact, the signs seem to speed up speech production at which point the signs drop out.

Finally, it has been suggested that for children with comprehension problems, seeing the sign in addition to hearing the word gives them an enhanced opportunity to develop understanding. Signing provides the bridge to speaking for children with language delays. It not only facilitates speech, but provides the child with a way to communicate. For children with language delays, it is imperative there be a way for parents and children to interact. When a child speaks or signs, parents respond with more sophisticated language, which is how children learn. When a child cannot initiate or respond, the parent may stop trying to continue the conversation or become more didactic. In the latter case, the naturalness of communication is replaced with parents trying to teach children to label, that is, "What's this? What's this?"

One little boy with autism spectrum disorder (ASD) had a few signs when he joined TOTalk. By the end of the semester (14 weeks), he was able to combine two signs or a sign plus a word to make phrases. He may never be fully verbal, but with signs and words, he can communicate his needs, likes, and dislikes.

Did You Know?

"If you think about making a sign, that visual icon stays in front of you longer than the word. Speech is very fast."

— Dr. Susan Hendler Lederer

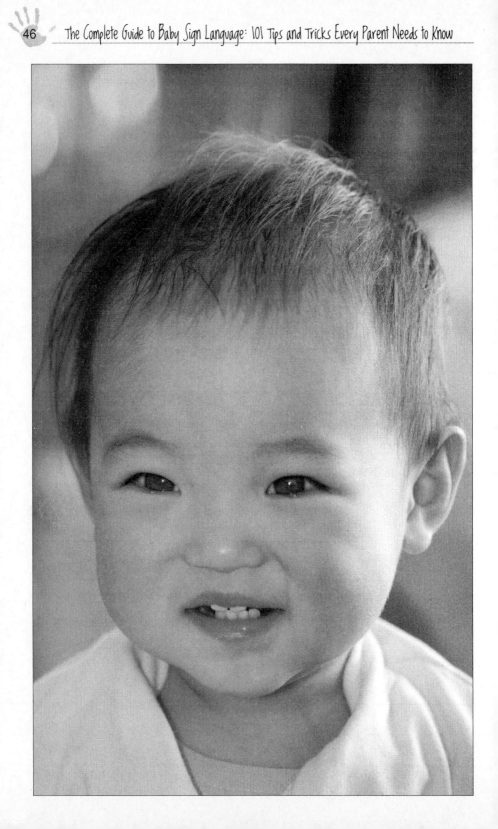

Chapter Three

Get Started Now — Learn Sign Language for Yourself

You have made the decision to use sign language with your baby. But before you make the commitment to teach your baby sign language, you need to learn a few signs yourself. It is important that you realize that you do not need to be proficient in ASL to communicate with your preverbal baby through sign language.

Teach Yourself Sign Language

You can learn just a few simple signs to get started. Begin by integrating them into your daily routine. By practicing the basic need signs, such as "more," and "diaper change," it will help you begin to master these signs yourself and, at the same time, demonstrate them to your baby. If you had a hard time learning a foreign language in high school or college, do not fret. Sign language is visual and is best learned by repetition.

Give yourself some practice tests when you find yourself with a few spare moments. Go to sign language Web sites, such as **www.ASLpro.com** or **www.aslDeafined.com**, to familiarize yourself with the way signs are performed. Learn five signs. It might be best to do this first thing in the morning when your mind is fresh and most alert. You should then make an effort to make these signs during the day when you utter the words. Find yourself seeking sentences where you can incorporate your new signs. For example, if you learned the sign for "banana," offer one to your baby, and when you say the word, make the sign. If you forget how to make a sign, check back to see how it is performed correctly. After using the sign more frequently, it will become easier to remember.

Get Educated

Over the last decade or so, many people have accepted the use of sign language in the hearing population, especially with babies. There are classes, books, and people who teach true ASL signs for the words your child will most likely need to use to communicate with you in his early years. However, there are certified "baby sign" instructors who teach the baby sign language that was created by Dr. Linda Acredolo and Dr. Susan Goodwyn. These signs, often simplified to make it easier for babies to make the gestures, are used in classes around the country to teach preverbal babies to communicate with their parents. However, if you are looking to groom a bilingual child, it is wise to stick to ASL or at least graduate to that once your baby gets the hang of using sign language gestures to communicate with you.

Tip:

"If I as a parent were picking and choosing what signs to get to know first, I would say get to know your baby, and what your baby is really motivated to say."

— Dawn Babb Prochovnic, founder of SmallTalk Learning

Learn Basic Signs

Practice makes perfect. To a newborn, you will likely utter the word "more" 20 times in one day. You ask your baby, "Do you want more milk?" or "Do you want to play more?" And, yes, "diaper change" is now a phrase that occurs in every other sentence. Say these words over and over again, and make the sign every time you utter these words. The repetition will help you learn this visual language and master the signs long before your baby will begin to use them. This will allow you to establish confidence in your signing and let it become second nature for you to sign these words during your daily routine. If you are an overachiever, teach yourself five to ten signs a week. There is no harm in showing your baby more signs than he needs or will use. Plus, it will help you become more familiar with the language. If you start teaching your baby sign language from the time he is born, you likely have between six and 18 months before he signs back to you. Do not be hard on yourself. If you mistakenly sign "milk" when you meant to sign "more," that does not mean your child will learn the wrong sign. Just correct yourself and move on.

Tip:

"When your child wakes up in the morning, and she stands in her crib, you can say, 'Mommy is here,' and do the sign for 'Mommy' again and again, until she learns the sign for 'Mommy.'"

— Nancy Barnett, sign language teacher and owner of Butterfly Hands in Shaker Heights, Ohio

CASE STUDY: PAUL FUGATE AND MERCY GONZALEZ

Cofounders of ASL Deafined, LLC
P.O. Box 214199
Auburn Hills, Michigan 48321
(248) 275-9728
info@aslDeafined.com

Having always been fascinated that you can communicate with someone who cannot hear, Paul Fugate decided to pursue a career in sign language interpreting, and became a teacher for deaf people. Mercy Gonzalez, who has worked with the deaf community for the past 15 years in various settings, was also interested in sign language from a young age. The pair created a Web site that teaches anyone sign language.

Our Web site includes linguistics, a 3,000-word video dictionary, activities, a personalized progress chart, and much more. Our motto for **ASLDeafined.com** is "Education, one person at a time." On ASL Deafined, all of the videos are clear, concise, and slow. ASL Deafined is one of the first Web sites of its kind.

Children learn sign language vocabulary, ASL grammar structure, and spelling both in English and sign language. They learn how to maneuver the Web site. The parents whom we come into contact with have subscribed to the site. Without exception, each of them has expressed a deep appreciation for such a resource. We are very realistic that parents can teach their babies sign language; we are all born with the ability to learn any language. When we do not use those skills, we lose them.

We are hopeful that everyone will learn some sign language to be able to communicate with anyone who is deaf. There is such a need for individuals to be able to communicate with everyone he or she encounters. Our long-term goals for ASL Deafined are to continue to offer a fresh Web site with many activities of retention for everyone to learn sign language. **ASLDeafined.com** is here to stay for a long, long time.

Tips for Teaching Yourself Sign Language

There are several ways to help yourself learn sign language. By following these steps, you can teach yourself all you need to know to begin early communication with your child:

Step No. 1

- Make the commitment to learning sign language. If you have decided to teach yourself sign language, do just that.

- Once you have made a commitment to yourself, make sure your partner is on board with your signing. It helps to use sign language with another adult to foster your learning and master signs that you will, in turn, teach your baby.

Step No. 2

- Set aside time each day to review signs you have taught yourself earlier that day.

- Refer to the sign language dictionary in the back of the book to help you master all the ASL signs you will need to communicate with your baby.

Step No. 3

- After you learn a sign, think of at least two ways to integrate it into your daily routine.

- If you teach yourself the sign for "all done," think of how you will illustrate this sign to your child, and help him understand the meaning of the sign as well as how to make it. For example, plan to use the sign "all done" when you ask your son, "Are you all done with your breakfast?" Also, plan to use it when he has made a mess of himself playing outside in the dirt. Say to him, "You are all done now, and we are going inside to get cleaned up."

• Practice the sign with your partner as well. If he or she is on board with signing — or, even better, learning along with you — you will create a signing household very conducive to your child's interest in ASL.

Step No. 4

• Keep teaching yourself new signs, but do not avoid practicing the ones you already know.

• Get in the habit of signing words you are saying.

• When you do not know a sign, look it up; this will help you increase your vocabulary. Before you know it, your signing vocabulary will be more then 50 words.

• One month later, your sign language vocabulary may double or triple, depending on the level of dedication you have for learning this visual language.

Chapter Four

How and When Can I Begin to Teach My Infant Sign Language?

Whether you are starting from birth, or you are introducing it to your 2-year-old who is speech delayed, it is never too late to teach the fundamentals of ASL to your child. There are many schools of thought as to how to begin to expose your baby to sign language, but ASL enthusiasts and teachers agree that between 6 and 18 months of age is the right time to integrate signing into your daily routine. This is when your baby cannot say the words to express what she wants to tell you, but she knows what she wants. Because most babies begin to talk between 10 and 18 months, it is the perfect time to allow them to not only use sign language to communicate with you, but to help you better understand their early words.

Tip:

"Do not think of it as teaching your child something. Instead, think of it as making language more accessible to them. You signed to interact in a fun way with your baby and make language more accessible."

— Lora Heller, founding director of Baby Fingers LLC

"Mommy/Daddy and Me" Classes

If watching DVDs and using flashcards is not working to help both you and your baby communicate via sign language, a "parent and me" class might be the remedy you are seeking. If you look in the phone book, search the Web, or inquire at the library or local daycare centers, you are bound to find some type of baby sign language class for moms and tots in your area. Though there may be some classes that use true ASL signs, others will focus on modified signs for babies. But all will give you the inspiration to use sign language in your daily life. Often, these classes are held in six- to eight-week intervals for sessions that last between a half-hour and one hour. The benefits are a group-learning environment where you can share your early sign language experiences with other parents who are trying to accomplish the same task you are: better and earlier two-way communication with your baby.

The class environment also presents a setting where babies learn to sign in a fun way. Most classes will use songs, books, and a host of props — from balls to puppets — to introduce sign language to you and your baby. For example, in Lora Heller's New York City-based Baby Fingers classes, the teacher will begin class with a song. The class participants will make signs for the words in the song, and the teacher will explain to parents how to continue to use the signs learned in class at home.

Most parents should know that if you attend classes with a child under 2 years old, it is not likely she will be signing at the end of your six-week session. This is why many parents will repeat the class for two or three sessions. The repetition helps you learn sign language better and continues your baby's exposure to it. Also, keep in mind that if you only attend a class and do not sign at home, your baby will not learn sign language. The class is simply for you and your baby to learn new signs.

CASE STUDY: NANCY BARNETT

Sign Language Teacher, Butterfly Hands
22088 Rye Road
Shaker Heights, Ohio 44122
(216) 577-7361
nancy.butterflyhands@gmail.com

After 20 years as an educational ASL interpreter, Nancy Barnett was burnt out in this career. She decided to start her own business, Butterfly Hands, where she teaches sign language in a daycare setting. Though she also teaches "Mommy and me" classes at a local public library, she enjoys teaching children in a daycare setting.

I am amazed at the ability of very young children to focus and learn so quickly. I have learned what is required to keep their attention: In my classes, I use many props, including puppets, books, flannel boards, and music. It has been very rewarding to facilitate communication between parents and their children.

I have had many parents tell me that using sign language has helped their children to become more confident and assimilate into the daycare setting more quickly. Parents have also reported that many temper tantrums have been halted due to the child's being able to make their needs known by signing. One parent of a child named Sofia wrote that "We have noticed so much growth in Sofia's confidence, and her language skills are even more impressive. One of the things that we feel helped with this was your sign language class on Tuesdays. We have noticed Sofia using and even teaching us signs for everything from colors and fruits to commands to Mom and Dad."

I have had typically developing children who are painfully shy, or who have difficulty separating from their parents, emerge from their shells with sign language. They become more self-confident and exhibit a sense of mastery.

I always tell parents to remember that our goal is to alleviate frustration, not create it. Learning sign language should be a happy, positive experience — one that can strengthen the parent-child bond. I urge parents not to correct their children's signs before the age of 3 and to keep the lessons fun and engaging. I also inform them to be realistic in their expectations of what a very young child can master. It is my goal to share ASL with families who wish to enhance their children's development and perhaps learn to communicate with their hearing- impaired or language-delayed peers.

Teaching Techniques

The more ways you integrate signing into your daily life, the more likely your baby will begin to use sign language to communicate with you. The following are a few ways to add signing into your daily activities:

- If you can add signing into the activities you already do with your baby, it is likely your baby will see this as the norm and will probably begin to sign more easily.

- If you sing every night to your baby, then start signing while you sing. Singing is soothing for your baby, and now you can make it interactive and more playful than before by adding signs.

- Sign where and when it feels comfortable for you and your baby. Do what works for you personally; the way to figure out what works for you is by trial and error. There is no rule of thumb for creating a successful little signer.

How Many Signs Should I Introduce at a Time?

There are two schools of thought in this realm: Sign every word relevant to your child's world so you are actually teaching her ASL, or sign just a few key words that will allow your child to learn these signs that will help her communicate her early needs and feelings to you. Both methods are equally efficient. It also depends on how you want to use sign language. Do you want a tool to communicate with your preverbal, hearing baby? Do you want her to simply give you a reason for why she is unhappy or happy? Or are you looking to create a bilingual child? If it is the latter, signing as many words as possible is truly effective.

You may ask yourself: Is there such a thing as signing too much? Will this confuse your baby? Will she be overwhelmed by sign language? This would not likely be the case, but it all depends on how fluent you are in sign language. If you are fluent in the language and want to use it specifically as a second language in your household, it is not going to hurt your baby in any way. In fact, if you are learning alongside her, then do what works for you, and she will follow suit.

Did You Know?

"Babies who are going to sign 'more' will sign the word 'more' for everything. That is typical language development called cognitive development. Once a child learns a cow says, 'moo,' they are likely to call every animal a 'moo.' It is over-generalization of language, so they will do that with the signs the same way they do it with language."

— Lora Heller, founding director of Baby Fingers LLC

Six-Month Timeline for Teaching Your Baby Sign Language

As discussed in previous chapters, you may start signing with your baby at birth, but it would be remarkable if she started to sign back before the age of 6 months. Usually, babies are exposed to sign language just as they are introduced to any other language. After a while of signing with your baby, many parents will start to think to themselves, "Am I doing this wrong? Maybe I am not using sign language enough. Am I making enough eye contact with her when I sign?" You are not doing anything wrong, because signing should be done at your own pace. It is simply that your baby is not yet ready to sign. Just like she will begin to walk when she is able and ready, she will sign when she is confident doing it.

Although every child will learn to sign at her own speed, there are certain patterns parents can expect to develop as they teach their baby sign language. The following is a six-month plan to guide you through this time period of teaching to your baby or toddler sign language:

Month No. 1

You have decided to teach your baby sign language, so you bought this book and maybe visited some Web sites where you have taught yourself some basic signs.

Tips: Choose signs that will help you communicate with your baby and are relevant to her world. If you start teaching a baby the signs for the things she will do in her life, such as eat, play, and get a diaper change, she is more likely to be receptive to the visual symbol you are showing her. To your 6 month old, "clean up your room" means nothing to her. On the other hand, that sign language phrase would have much more meaning to your 2 year old, who certainly may need to learn the meaning of "clean up."

What to expect from your child: Depending on the age of your child when you begin signing, she will become receptive to these signs even if she does not attempt to make them. She is receptive if she is simply watching. A smile or a simple coo when you make the sign for milk or eat will also tell you that she listening and learning.

Month No. 2

You have introduced sign language to your child, who now sees this as a regular part of her daily routine. Mommy and Daddy's using their hands to communicate is not a foreign concept, but instead it is welcomed and recognized by your baby. This month, you want to work on your signing vocabulary, even if your child has yet to make a single sign. Begin using the lesson plans that follow in this chapter to help introduce new signs to your baby.

Tips: Remember to look in your child's eyes when you sign. Look to see that she is looking at the sign and at you. Your job is to make sure you are making the signs and she is watching you make them.

What to expect from your child: By the end of Month 2, you should be using at least 20 signs that you have incorporated into your daily routines. If your baby is 6 months old or older, she may have picked up the sign for "more" and is using it over and over again. Although you are signing "happy" every opportunity you get, your child may only want to sign "more." Maybe that is the sign most relevant to your child, or the easiest one for her to make. Continue signing, and do not stop.

Month No. 3

If one sign a week has been successful for you, now begin to implement a "sign of the day" at least three times a week. In this time period, you should teach signs for colors, animals, and objects in your baby's world. *Refer to the lesson plan that follows this timeline.*

Tips: Teach image-based signs that your child will be excited to learn (like "helicopter" or "telephone"), and give this sign special attention in your daily routine.

What to expect from your child: Your child will be enthusiastic to learn the sign of the day. She may attempt to make the sign, but it might not be perfect. Her sign approximation, however, is a milestone. Any time your baby attempts to make a sign, be proud of her and offer some type of positive reinforcement. You may also wish to teach the sign for "proud."

Month No. 4

By now, your child may be using sign language to tell you she likes red apples or cannot wait to get to sleep. But do not stop here; keep going. This month, you should increase your own signing vocabulary in order to make it more accessible to your child. Think about where she is developmentally; if she is cruising (the precursor to walking), teach her the signs for the items in her view.

Tips: Expand your child's signing vocabulary to two-word phrases by teaching her signs for descriptive words. If your child signs "bear" every night before bed, she may want her brown bear in her crib when she goes to sleep. Put emphasis on the words "brown" and "bear" when you say it, and make the sign for "brown," along with "bear."

What to expect from your child: If your child is not signing yet, she is likely eager to do so. By signing words that are fun and exciting to her, such as the words for some favorite toys, she will be more likely to use the signs when she wants you to get that toy off the shelf for her, and may very well be doing so at this point.

Month No. 5

If your child has begun to sign as well as speak, or simply make an attempt at signing, it is time to use sign language to help your baby develop her verbal abilities.

Tips: If your child is making five or more signs, use them to facilitate her speaking skills. If your child says "ba ba" and makes the sign for milk, ask: "Do you want your bottle of milk?" Make both the signs for "bottle" and "milk," and emphasize the pronunciation of "bottle," instead of simply mimicking her. Do not facilitate the baby talk. Promote the proper words and signs for what she wants.

What to expect from your child: If your child's words are unclear as she begins to speak, sign language will allow you to understand what she is trying to say. In addition, her words will come easier, and she will be less frustrated.

Month No. 6

Last month, you were working to help your child sign her early words. This month — and in coming months, as she begins to speak more clearly — use two- and three-word sentences. Also, use the signs for the words in the sentence.

Tips: Your child may be tempted to drop the signs for the words she says. The way to continue and grow her sign language abilities is for you to make an effort to initiate and teach her more sign language each day.

What to expect from your child: Your child will now be using signs and words together. Sometimes, the sign may not match the word, or her signs may not be perfect. But as she says a new word, she will be eager to learn new signs for her new vocabulary words.

25 Lesson Plans for 52 Weeks of Teaching Sign Language to Your Baby

Now that your child is both using sign language and speaking, it is time to home in on her signing skills. Following are lesson plans you can follow over a one-year time frame. The following 25 lessons will prove beneficial to use with any child over the age of 2 years. The goal of these lessons is to teach your child new signs, show her to integrate them into a daily routine, and demonstrate how to continue to use sign language to communicate with people.

The 25 lessons need to be repeated several times over a 52-week period. Choose to implement one, three, or seven per week, mix them up, and add your own special touches and elements to them if you wish. But make sure to repeat each one at least once using the same signs, so your child will use her memory skills to recall the signs she has learned.

Lesson No. 1

Goal: Teach new sign language vocabulary.

What you will need: A large bin, toy chest, or basket, as well as five of her favorite toys.

How it works:

1. Put five of your child's favorite toys in a covered basket, bin, or toy chest.

2. Tell her to go see what is inside the chest.

3. As she takes out a stuffed duck, say, "duck," and make the sign for the word. Do this with each toy.

4. Repeat the game with the some toys every few days to see how well she remembers the signs for the words.

Lesson No. 2

Goal: Teach the signs for different foods.

What you will need: A refrigerator full of food.

How it works:

1. Open the refrigerator and ask your child, "What is inside?"

2. Say "food," and make the sign for food.

3. Pick five foods your child likes. Examples: jelly, bread, apple, pizza, and juice.

4. Take the items out of the refrigerator, and let her help carry them to the table so she is included in this fun activity.

5. Line the items up on the table.

6. Ask her what each item is, and as she says the word for each food item, show her the sign.

7. Have her repeat the sign and the words along with you.

Lesson No. 3

Goal: Integrate sign language into familiar routines.

What you will need: A favorite storybook.

How it works:

1. Read your child's favorite storybook. Sit next to her on the floor, couch, or bed, and hold the book open with one hand.

2. Use your other hand to make the signs for the words relevant in the book. The book will hold your baby's interest.

3. She will look at the sign, hear the word, and simultaneously see the book illustration. Books are a great way to reinforce signs because of the pairing of visual images with the signs.

Lesson No. 4

Goal: Practice expressive signing.

What you will need: Pictures of people (you can cut these out of magazines or print them off the Internet) making happy, sad, and mad faces.

How it works:

1. Tell your child to guess which expression or emotion the person in the photo is likely experiencing.

2. Ask, "Is the little girl in the picture happy or sad?"

3. Ask your child to not only answer, but to use the signs she already knows to respond to.

Lesson No. 5

Goal: Teach the meaning of words in different ways.

What you will need: Props that illustrate the words you will teach. For example, if you are teaching the word "milk," you will need a bottle of milk and a book that features a cow.

How it works:

1. To teach the word "milk," you will obviously sign the word every time you give your child milk. But if you are reading a book that has a cow in it, talk about how the cow makes milk and sign the word for "milk" as well.

2. To teach the sign for "more," ask your baby — in a variety of circumstances — "Do you want more?"

3. To teach the sign for "diaper change," make the sign when you are changing your baby's diaper. But make sure to say the words: "I am going to change your diaper now." When you think she needs a diaper change, ask, "Do you need a diaper change?"

4. To teach the sign for "All done," ask your baby after she has eaten, "Are you all done?" and make the sign.

5. Use it again when she finished with her bath: "Ashley is all done with her bath now."

Lesson No. 6

Goal: Use signing to promote good hygiene.

What you will need: Soap, shampoo, and a warm bath.

How it works:

1. Put your child in the bathtub for her regular bath. Instead of simply playing with bath toys, talk about the things she sees in the shower.

2. Every time you say a word, such as shampoo, towel, or soap, make the sign, and ask her to make the sign along with you.

3. Talk about the purpose of the bath — to get clean — and how you wash your hair and face.

4. Repeat the signs for each item being used, such as "soap" and "shampoo." Then also make the signs for her body parts, such as "hair," "face," "feet," as she is washing them.

Lesson No. 7

Goal: Learn the sign language alphabet needed for fingerspelling.

What you will need: The sign language illustration dictionary at the back of this book. *See Appendix A.*

How it works:

1. Tell your child you are going to teach her how to say her ABCs in sign language.

2. As you sing the ABC song aloud, show her the sign for each letter of the alphabet.

3. Then, during each of the next 26 days, tell her she will make the "letter sign of the day." For example, Monday will be "A" day and Tuesday will be "B" day.

4. During each day, find as many objects you can point out to your child that begins with that word. For example, ask your child, "Do you want an apple? Apple begins with 'A.'" Then make the sign for the letter "A."

Lesson No. 8

Goal: Learn the signs for colors.

What you will need: Paint in primary colors, paper, and a smock for your child.

How it works:

1. Take a paintbrush and dip it in your child's favorite-colored paint. Allow her to paint using only that color. Ask, "What color is it?" Then show her the sign for that particular color.

2. Repeat this with as many colors as you desire, mixing them to make colors for which you may not have the paint. For example, mix red and blue to make purple. When you do this, explain you are mixing the colors. Make the sign for "red" and "blue" when you use each color, and the sign for "purple" once it is created.

Lesson No. 9

Goal: Allow your child to learn new signs through discovery.

What you will need: Plastic eggs and items she can hold, such as crayons, stickers, and small toys.

How it works:

1. Fill up about ten plastic eggs with different items.

2. Hide them in spots around your house or in the backyard.

3. Give your child a basket and tell her to put each egg she finds in the basket.

4. After she has collected all the eggs, open each one individually.

5. Ask her what is inside each one.

6. As she says the word for each item she finds, show her the signs for the words.

7. Ask her to make the signs with you.

Lesson No. 10

Goal: Learn new signs by expressing creativity.

What you will need: Paper, markers, child's scissors, a magazine, and a glue stick.

How it works:

1. Ask your child to choose and cut out pictures from a magazine that she likes.

2. Ask your child to make a collage with these photos. Before she glues each one onto the page, she needs to identify each item and make the sign for it.

3. Ask her to explain what the person in the picture is doing. For example, if it is a photo of a baby eating ice cream, make the sign for "baby" and "ice cream."

Lesson No. 11

Goal: Practice fingerspelling.

What you will need: A list of the names of all the people in your family. Choose ten.

How it works:

1. Tell your child you are thinking of someone with gray hair and a beard. Can she guess whom it is?

2. When she says, "Uncle John," for example, show her how to fingerspell his name.

3. Repeat this with as many family member names as you desire to get your child into the habit of fingerspelling.

Lesson No. 12

Goal: Learn signs for shapes.

What you will need: Colorful construction paper, a pencil, and child's scissors.

How it works:

1. Cut out a variety of shapes, such as rectangles, triangles, octagons, and hexagons.

2. Place them in a pot, bowl, or basket.

3. Ask your child to reach her hand into the basket without looking to pick out a shape.

4. Once she has it, ask her to identify the shape both verbally and with a sign you will teach her at this time.

Lesson No. 13

Goal: Teach your child the signs for apparel items.

What you will need: Underwear, shirt, pants, shoes, socks, hat, gloves, scarf, and coat.

How it works:

1. Tell your child you are going to play the dress-up game. Begin with putting on her underwear, and progress to each item of clothing.

2. As you put each item on your child, say the words, "I am now putting your shirt on," and make the sign for each clothing item.

3. Once she is all dressed with a hat, coat, gloves, and scarf, begin to remove the outerwear and reinforce those signs by making them again as each item is removed.

Lesson No. 14

Goal: Discover the signs for animals.

What you will need: Directions to your local zoo.

How it works:

1. Take your child to a local zoo and show her the signs for every animal she sees. Make the process fun. Ask, "Do you know what kind of animal that is?"

2. If she says "monkey," ask her, "Can you make the sign for 'monkey'?" If she says no, model the sign for her.

3. Visit the exhibits a second time, either that day or the following week, then ask her to make the signs for the animals as she encounters each one.

Lesson No. 15

Goal: Learn numbers and signs for numbers.

What you will need: A ruler, calculator, flashcards, or a book with the numbers 1 to 20.

How it works:

1. Tell your child you are going to play a counting game.

2. As you teach her to count, sign each number, starting with the number 1. If she already knows how to count to 20, go to 25 or a higher number.

3. Use this exercise weekly during your 52-week plan. Each time, add on five more numbers, along with the signs for each new number.

4. Not only will your child grow in her signing vocabulary, but she will learn how to count to a higher number each time.

Lesson No. 16

Goal: Learn the meaning of opposites through sign language.

What you will need: Photos or objects to illustrate the words "hot," "cold," "near," "far," "big," "little," "short," and "tall."

How it works:

1. Take your items for "hot" and "cold" — they could simply be your kitchen sink.

2. Turn on the hot water and explain that it is too hot to touch. Make sure she is in a safe distance away from it, then make the sign for "hot."

3. Repeat the same action with the cold water. In this case, before the water gets too cold, let your child touch the water so she can feel it is cold.

4. Take your objects for "near" and "far," which could simply be a pair of shoes.

5. Place one near your child and the other one far away across the room.

6. Explain that one is "near," and make the sign for "near." Do the same with "far."

7. Take the objects for "big" and "little." This can simply be one of your shoes and one of hers.

8. Show her the difference in size, and when you say "big" and "little," make the signs for the words.

9. Do the same for "short" and "tall," which could simply be the two of you.

Lesson No. 17

Goal: Teach your child the words and signs for the months of the year.

What you will need: A calendar.

How it works:

1. Begin with January, and ask your child questions to help her guess the month you are talking about. For example, "In what month might we build a snowman?"

2. Go through each month on the calendar and show her the sign for each month.

3. You may want to reinforce these signs through the year by asking your child several times within each month, "What month is it?"

4. Then say, "Can you sign it for me, too?"

Lesson No. 18

Goal: Forecasting weather with sign language.

What you will need: A window your child can reach.

How it works:

1. Play the "weather of the day" game with your child each day, or at least a few days per week.

2. Ask your child to go to the window and look outside.

3. Ask, "What is the weather like? Is it hot or cold? Sunny? Windy? Rainy?"

4. When she replies with the one-word description of the weather, make the sign.

5. Then give your little signing weather forecaster a thumbs-up for a job well done.

Lesson No. 19

Goal: Teach your child the words and signs for the seasons of the year.

What you will need: Either photos or the actual items for leaves, sand, snow, and rain.

How it works:

1. Tell your child she will learn the seasons of the year. Look at photos or the items you have collected and, with each one, talk about the seasons.

2. Put a special focus on the current season. The following is an example for the season of autumn.

3. Show your child a leaf, or go outside and collect leaves that have fallen from the trees.

4. Explain that the season "autumn" is when you will see the most leaves falling from trees.

5. Make the sign for autumn.

6. Talk about wearing sweaters and warmer clothing in the fall. Talk about the sports, such as soccer, that can be played outside in the autumn.

7. Make the sign for autumn every time you say the word.

Lesson No. 20

Goal: Learn time with sign language.

What you will need: A clock.

How it works:

1. Tell your child she is going to learn how to tell time.

2. When it is noon, show her where the hands on the clock will signify this time.

3. Make the signs for 12 o'clock. Do this for each hour of the day.

4. As your child gets older, you can add the half-hour.

5. Incorporate this lesson regularly into your day by asking your child at a certain time, "What time is it?"

6. When she tells you, ask her to sign the time to you.

7. Now, she is learning how to tell time and increasing her sign language vocabulary at the same time.

Lesson No. 21

Goal: Allow your child to sign what she sees.

What you will need: To keep your child alert on a walk through your neighborhood.

How it works:

1. Tell your child you are going outside to play the see-and-sign game.

2. She should tell you what she sees as you take a leisurely stroll through your neighborhood.

3. As she verbalizes words of objects, such as "houses," "trees," and "birds," either teach her the sign for the words or ask her to show you them if she already knows how to make them.

Lesson No. 22

Goal: Allow your child to sign what she hears.

What you need: Objects that make distinct sounds, such as a tambourine, bells, and drums.

How it works:

1. Sit your child in the middle of a room with her back facing you.

2. Tell her not to look.

3. Tell her to identify the sounds she hears with words.

4. Make a sound, such as a bell ringing.

5. Once she says the words "bell" or "ring," make sure you are in her view and ask her to sign the words for you, or show her the signs for the words.

Lesson No. 23

Goal: Allow your child to sign what she feels.

What you will need: A very attentive eye and listening ear.

How it works:

1. This is when you let your child dictate to you what signs she will make. It is not a lesson you may intentionally initiate, but one that is more of a reaction to your child's needs.

2. For example, if your child begins to cry, ask what is wrong. If she begins to cry more intensely where words will not likely come, ask her to sign what is wrong for you.

3. Maybe she will sign the word "hurt" and point to her head. This would let you know she is crying because she bumped her head.

4. Initiate her feeling signs any time she may look quiet, sad, or even happy, and you simply do not know why.

Lesson No. 24

Goal: Allow your child to sign what she wants. This is using sign language as a true second language.

What you will need: To be attentive to her needs.

How it works:

1. If your child points to an object but either does not yet say the word or simply fails to use it, ask her to sign it for you.

2. Get her in the habit of initiating sign language when she wants you to do something for her by always asking what she wants. If she says, "I want ice cream," ask her to sign it as well.

3. Her reward for using sign language can be what she is asking for. However, let her know that will not always be the case. If she asks for ice cream right before dinner, you can sign back, "After dinner."

Lesson No. 25

Goal: Use props to stimulate your child's interest in sign language.

What you will need: Various props, which can include a puppet, flannel board, or flashcards.

How it works:

- *Puppets* — Kids love puppet people and animals that appear to talk to them. Purchase a signing puppet that allows you to stick your arm through so your hands can make the signs.

- *Flannel boards* — Any colorful, illustrated boards with the signs and objects pictured on them can be helpful because the child will see the images and watch you illustrate the sign.

- *Flashcards* — This is a great way to introduce signs. You can use any set of flashcards that have illustrations and words, and there also are cards you can buy that add an illustration of the sign for the word pictured on that card. In addition, you should also demonstrate how the sign is done for reinforcement.

Chapter Five

Sign Language Teaching Tools

Make Learning Fun

The only rule of teaching your baby sign language is that it remains fun for both you and your child. So what are fun activities for you and your baby? Playtime and singing will rank No. 1 on your child's priority list. Parents and sign language teachers alike enjoy connecting sights and song while teaching sign language. The following are some great songs — those we all know and love — that can help your baby learn signs relevant to her world:

"Old MacDonald Had a Farm": Illustrate the signs for every animal in the song, such as "pig," "cow," "horse," and "chicken." As your child begins to learn the signs for each animal, add new ones — even if they were not originally in the classic children's song. For example, "...and on his farm, he had a frog..."

"Twinkle, Twinkle Little Star": This song is great for teaching ASL through repetition. Model the signs for "twinkle," "sky," and "star" as you say each word in the song.

"Itsy-Bitsy Spider": Teach the signs for "water," "spider," "rain," and "washed."

"Wheels on the Bus": This catchy tune already has hand gestures in it. It is a great sign language tool to provide an interactive environment and to simultaneously communicate that sign language is enjoyable for your baby. Teach your child the signs for "wheels," "bus," "round," "town," "wipers," "people," "driver," and "babies."

If these classic baby tunes do not fit in with your signing repertoire, sign to your favorites. If you add music to your household, this can be an opportunity for you to sing along and add signing. For example, if you buy a kids' CD, have these songs playing when you and your baby are interacting together during the day. As you look into your baby's eyes and sing and sign the relevant words, you will see your baby enjoying the music and learning the signs at the same time.

Did You Know?

"Music itself enhances language. Music is such a motivator for babies. If you are signing while you are signing, babies are more likely to look at you, and be interested in what it is you are doing."

— Lora Heller, signing instructor

Signing as Structured Play

Sign language can be taught through other structured play activities. The following is a list of common games you can use sign language to play:

- **Where is baby?:** As soon as your baby starts the discovery phase, he will begin it with his own body. You can play "Where is Baby's

Nose?" As your baby touches his nose, make the sign for "nose." You can do this with the following body parts: "feet," "head," "eyes," "mouth," "arms," and "legs."

- **Playground activities:** Whether you live in a big city or a suburb, there are so many signing opportunities in structured play that can occur outdoors. If you put your baby on a swing, push him while he is facing you.

- **Hide and seek:** This all-time childhood favorite game can be an opportunity to sign new words to your child. You can find the opportunity to integrate the signs for the following words and phrases into a game of hide and seek. Use the signs for the following words and phrases: "find," "you," "hide," "Where are you?" and "I can see you."

> **Tip:**
>
> "Sign in sequence so your baby knows what is coming. I would sign and say, 'We're going to change your diaper, so then you can play; it will be really fast.' I would do the signs for change, diaper, and play, so he knows it will not be an infinity before he gets off the changing table. A big part of a baby's life is routine, and when he knows what is coming next, it puts him at ease."
>
> — Cindy Santa Ana, owner of Sign Together with Cindy

Watching Your Baby Make Connections

We know babies have their own wants and needs. They know what they want; but again, they cannot use the words to tell us. Once your baby starts signing, he will use sign language to communicate to you about his world — not your world, filled with a neverending list of things to do, people to call, and the task of juggling work and parenthood. Parents often want to teach children signs that will be helpful in their parenting skills, such as "do not touch," "be careful," or "stop." But your child will not embrace these signs as well as the ones that have more meaning to him and his immediate wants and needs. In fact, he will be more eager to sign about his world, which consists of eating new foods, playing games, learning about what these interesting objects in his view are, and how to do things, such as roll over, crawl, and walk. He might also use sign language to let you know he likes a new food or the big pillow you just bought for your living room sofa.

If a parent becomes lax in signing as the child begins to talk, the child often follows suit and drops the signing as well. Children will stop signing at different points in their lives. For example, if a child is learning to walk, he has something physical going on where he may need to use his hands to hold on top items, such as furniture. For this reason, the child may neglect to sign at this point in his life. It is the parent's job to continue to make signing fun and relevant. If your child is holding onto the couch while cruising, once he plops back onto the floor, ask him if he wants more or is hungry using both spoken words and sign language. When he is still and not concentrating on another activity, he will be more likely to sign back to you.

CASE STUDY: DEEANNE L. LOWMAN

Parent from Hyattsville, Maryland
dlowman@foundryumc.org
www.foundryumc.org

DeeAnne L. Lowman is a minister for discipleship at Congregational Life Foundry United Methodist Church in Washington, D.C. She had taken a few sign language classes in the 1990s and wanted to use sign language to bridge the language gap between her son Max, who was ad-

opted from China in October 2008 at the age of 14 months, and his family in America. She used sign language to help him learn English, and it allowed him to communicate what he wanted and was feeling before he learned to speak and understand English words.

Many children adopted from other countries are not familiar with the English language. Often, adopted children are older than 1 year when their adopted parents take them home to America. This often is their first experience with the English language. The adoptive parents are faced with the difficult task of communicating with a child who has been spoken to in another language for the first year of his life.

We started signing with Max at 14 months old. Soon after, he did his first sign: "more." We assume that his foster family in China taught him that one. After that, we kept speaking and signing, and he caught on quickly and mimicked our signs accurately. We were aware that Max probably had few English-speaking folks around him before we came into his life. We wanted him to be able to communicate his needs and desires to us.

The next two signs were "da da" and "ma ma." Because of sign language, we knew what he wants and needs, especially when it comes to food. He will sign "banana" or "apple." We could understand him, and he could make himself understood. This was essential during our time bonding with Max. He needed to know that we were there for him and could meet his needs.

We had him evaluated by the Maryland Infants and Toddlers program, and they said that his receptive language was very good. They attributed some of this to the signing. At this point, he is only saying a few words at 21 months, but his words come out of his signing. Any English word he has said, he has signed first. He signs all the time, especially at mealtime. Once he has learned the sign, the word appears to come more easily to him when it does come. We are still signing the words he can say. Sometimes, though, he drops the sign after he can say the word.

We captured Max signing on video and posted it to our blog. We contacted folks who live out of town and let them know it was there for them to use. We use online video calls so people can see the signs to understand Max because they have learned the signs he knows. This has made a great deal of difference in his feelings about strangers and other folks he does not see very often. Some members of my congregation also sign with him, which is a cool way that he can feel included in the life of the church, even at his young age.

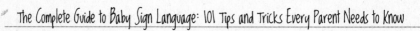

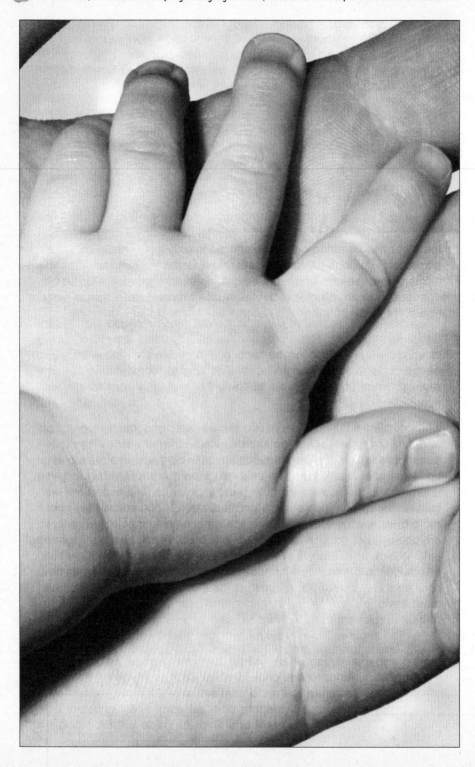

Guidelines for When and Where to Sign

Signing at home

Home is likely where the majority of your signing will occur. Though it might not feel right or may ignite unwanted questions and conversation when you are signing to your child at a family party, in contrast, at home you can induce a one-on-one dynamic with your child. Here, sign language can became the norm for you and your child if you foster it by using it on a continuous basis. This chapter and previous sections have mentioned how signing can be used during mealtime, bedtime, while singing, and during game playing, but what about while you are cleaning the house, or talking on the phone to Grandma? Use sign language like you would any other language to include your baby in the conversations in your world.

Signing in public

As your child gets older, signing in public can be used in several different ways and for various reasons. You can simply use it the same way you do at home. However, as your child grows, signing in public can be used as a "secret" communication tool between you and your child. While many people in the country will recognize the sign for "I love you," you will not find many people totally fluent in sign language in your daily travels. With this being said, sign language can be used when you and your child simply do not want anyone to know what you are conversing about. People who are fluent in other languages often do this around children when they simply think the conversation is not suitable. Sign language is used the same way. You can now tell your child from across the room to pull up her pants if they are falling down in sign language, or your child may sign to you that she really needs to use the bathroom in a crowded restaurant.

Group settings

In addition to taking the "parent-and-me" class approach, once you have exhausted all you can learn from one of these six- or eight-week sessions, you may want to form your own parent-signing group. Just like you would set up a playgroup of moms where mothers and fathers swap stories and kids play in the backyard, the same can be done with a signing focus. Often, these playgroups will grow out of sign language classes. However, if you never attended a sign language class, you can place an advertisement in your local newspaper or on parenting blog Web sites to entice other parents to join the group. Some of these Web sites include the following:

- **Parents Click Network:** This Web site connects parents in social networks of several interests: **www.parentsclick.com**

- **Families.com:** An online parenting resource: **http://parenting. families.com**

- **Empowering Parents:** A Web site for parenting advice: **http:// empoweringparents.com**

You can elect to be the group leader — at least for your first meeting — and select a theme, such as days of the week. When the mothers, fathers, or nannies arrive, you can hand out a list of the signs you will use in the playgroup that day and ask that they practice them at home. At some meetings, it would be useful to utilize props, such as toys and storybooks. In fact, to allow for participation, you can request that parents bring their children's favorite toys to the next gathering, and be prepared to illustrate the sign for that toy. Parents can take turns hosting the gatherings as they would any other type of playgroup. In addition, plan outings to parks and zoos, where the elements of these places can be used to illustrate signs for the children. For example, if the group is walking through a park, ask the children to pick up or point to one thing in the park for which they would like to learn the sign.

CASE STUDY: CINDY SANTA ANA

Sign Together with Cindy
2490 New Seabury Way
Chula Vista, California 91915
(619) 405-9386
signtogetherwithcindy@cox.net

Cindy Santa Ana learned some baby sign language when her firstborn was 8 months old. She enjoyed it so much, and found it to be such an effective means of communication, that she took classes at a local recreation center from a Sign2Me instructor. She repeated the classes when her second child was born and has now been using sign language for almost four years. She also has started her own business teaching babies sign language in December 2008. She teaches baby sign language in formal classes, story times at local libraries, and at a mommy & me class for preschoolers. She says she is particularly surprised at how well signing helps with the "terrible twos."

When children become frustrated and start acting out, signing "stop" or "no" can have more of an impact that just saying it. You can also sign to them and ask them what they want when they get mad, and it helps them to calm down. They use their signs to get the point across.

Babies will go through signing stages of amusement, then recognizing or understanding of what you are doing; then, they may attempt to sign or imitate you with or without success, then finally they start to sign and eventually you end up with a signing baby. This may take months, and some may even experience setbacks in signing while their baby is mastering another skill, such as cruising or walking.

Children exposed to sign language early in life will not only find it easy to learn ASL later, but they will find it easier to learn any language later. And it is not just for babies, either — keep up the learning as your child begins to speak, and you and your child can develop a second language together.

Benefits of Repetitive Signing

You have been signing with your baby for more than a year. She just started making signs and knows between five and 35 signs well. However, lack of usage of these signs will often cause a child to stop signing. For this reason, you need to engage in repetitive signing practices. Repetitive signing is essentially a process in which you make sure you use the same sign in several different ways during your daily activities. Sign language is not like riding a bicycle; if you do not use a particular sign for a period of time, it is likely you will forget how to make it. For this reason, use the signs you know with your child, and use them frequently.

Chapter Six

How Can I Use Sign Language to Prevent Tantrums and to Potty Train?

Tackling Tantrums Before They Occur

All babies and toddlers throw tantrums. These occur usually when you least expect them to, such as when you are walking out the door to go to your parents' house and are already late. They might happen for no particular reason, such as your child's shoes are too tight, or she just hates that bow you just stuck in her hair. These fits of what appear to be rage can last from anywhere between five minutes to an hour, and they often include uncontrollable crying, kicking, and screaming.

It is inevitable that these events will occur. In fact, many of your child's tantrums that occur early in life will stem from his frustration of not being able to communicate with you. The baby who knows sign language will avoid tantrums more often because he can tell his parent exactly what is wrong, using one sign.

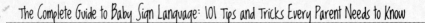

Exercises to Help Prevent or Calm a Tantrum Using Sign Language

Exercise No. 1

Goal: To initiate the use of sign language to prevent a tantrum.

How it works: Recognize that your child is not happy or is about to become frustrated. The key here is recognizing that your child is on the onset of feeling this way before he actually exhibits these emotions. Then, follow these steps:

1. Ask, "What is wrong?"

2. You may get a pout, or the beginning of tears.

3. Ask, "Can you tell me what is wrong?"

4. If he does not tell you in the next few seconds, say, "Can you sign what is wrong?"

5. Your child may soon make the sign for "broken" or "puppy."

6. At that point, you can take a look at his toy puppy and see that it needs new batteries or has other problems.

Exercise No. 2

Goal: Stop tantrums from getting worse with sign language.

How it works: If your child begins to cry and you are not aware of the reason why, follow these steps:

1. Ask, "Why are you crying?"

2. If he says nothing, but continues to cry, ask, "Can you sign what you are crying about?"

3. If he does not immediately make a sign, make the sign for what you suspect is wrong. For example, if he was playing outside, and you found him on the floor, say, "Did you fall down and get hurt?" Make the sign for "fall down," and "hurt" when you say them.

4. He may simply respond "yes" at this point. But if he shakes his head "no," say, "If you can not tell me what is wrong, will you sign it for me?"

5. In many cases, the child will make the sign to communicate what is wrong if he is accustomed to using ASL.

Exercise No. 3

Goal: Use signing to prevent an argument between you and your child.

How it works: It seems as if many children learn the fundamentals of arguing early in their lives. To avoid constant bickering with your child, initiate signing before a full-blown argument may ensue. For example:

1. If you tell your child to finish his dinner, and he says, "No, I'm not hungry," explain with both ASL and spoken words that there will be no dessert if he refuses to eat his dinner. The sign language reinforces what you are telling him and has him focused on you for the moment.

2. He may use sign language to sign back that he is "sick," "tired," or maybe changed his mind about eating and would like some fruit for dessert.

3. The sign language, in many cases, can help the two of you come to an understanding sooner because you are focused on each other and watching the signs.

Exercise No. 4

Goal: Use sign language to reprimand your child in public.

How it works: If your child is misbehaving in some way while on a play date, at a party, or at another public gathering, use sign language to reprimand him without embarrassing him.

1. When you see your child misbehaving, say his name. When he has made eye contact with you, sign "stop," or "no," without saying the words. This may be the only time you may opt to sign without using spoken words, and sign language becomes your secret language.

2. In many cases, your child will simply obey. If not, call his name again, and show intensity in your signing with eye contact and exaggerated movement.

3. If he still misbehaves, you can remove him from the situation. But in many cases, an intensely performed sign might be all you need in the situation.

Build Self-Esteem

Teaching your baby sign language allows you to provide him with the ability to do something that will make him proud. When he can sign "all done" after he has eaten dinner, and he sees the smile grow on your face because of this successful communication that has taken place, he gets a confidence boost. This is an integral part of growth and a good start on fostering a healthy childhood.

Here is a scenario to think about:

1. Your baby, who was never introduced to sign language, is 18 months old and cannot yet speak. He is walking around your backyard and stubs his toe on a rock. It starts to bleed inside his new white shoes. But all you see is that he walked right into dirt and a puddle with his brand-new white shoes. You say, "Why did you do that while wearing your new shoes?"

2. He thinks you are angry, but now his toe really starts to throb, and he starts to cry.

3. You do not know he is hurt. He is upset because not only did he hurt herself, but he cannot tell you.

4. He thinks he did something very wrong, and you are mad at him.

5. He is crying uncontrollably.

Here is the same scenario with a signing baby:

1. He walks in the dirt and stubs his toe on a rock in your backyard, wearing the brand-new white shoes.

2. He begins to cry.

3. You turn around, but before you can get mad about his shoes, he signs the word "hurt" and points to his foot.

4. You look down, take off his shoes, and see the toe bleeding.

5. You reward him for signing, and say (as well as sign) "Good job," and take him inside to bandage the toe.

6. He feels a sense of pride that he was able to tell you what was wrong, and a lengthy period of crying is avoided.

7. Your child's ability to sign also avoided any hurt feelings.

By building self-esteem through the use of sign language, you reduce any frustration your child may have that stems from a lack of communication with you. Because he can sign his wants and needs to you, he experiences less frustration, which translates into fewer tantrums and a more confident child who is eager to show Mom and Dad all the signs he can do.

To use sign language to help your child build self-esteem, try initiating one or more of the following self-esteem building exercises that can prove beneficial to any child:

Exercise No. 1

1. Ask your child to play the "I sign, you sign" game with you.

2. Ask him to make his favorite sign.

3. If he is already speaking, ask him to also say the word for this sign (this can range from anything from "milk" to "rubber ducky").

4. Next, you should illustrate a sign you know your child knows, and ask him what it is.

5. When he correctly guesses the sign, explain how proud you are of his signing abilities.

6. At the point when he is beaming with pride, repeat the game.

Exercise No. 2

1. Choose a sign your child likes to make.

2. Make this the "sign of the day," and tell him that he will get some type of reward (stickers or gold stars usually work well) every time he makes that sign on this day.

3. Rewards help build self-esteem because they show children they have done a good job.

Exercise No. 3

1. Watch sign language DVDs with your child or go to a Web site that allows your child to learn new signs.

2. Ask your child what sign he would like to learn today.

3. Let your child watch the way the sign is made.

4. Ask him to make the sign.

5. Once he makes the sign or attempts to make it, make a big deal about how well he was able to learn the new sign.

6. Find ways to incorporate this sign into your routine that day.

7. For example, if he chooses the sign for "shoe," ask your child to get his shoes. Make the sign for "shoes," and ask him to sign it as well.

8. Give him a reward every time he makes the sign.

Any time you give your child positive reinforcement, it builds self-esteem. Sign language allows you to have the perfect number of opportunities to tell your child he has done a good job. Just as if he would be praised for walking, reading, or getting his first soccer goal, positive reinforcement is a big part of language and is an essential ingredient to your child's self-esteem.

Signing to Potty Train

In your child's lifetime, you will teach him many useful things. Perhaps one of the most useful, yet difficult, things to teach your child is how to use the toilet. Though some parents will report potty training to be easy, others will recall this process as one of the most frustrating periods of toddlerhood. There are those children who simply do not want to potty train. In fact, they are perfectly content doing their business in their diaper, letting you know it has been done, and having you change it for them. But if you want your child to attend school, it is often required that he use the potty on his own.

Just as sign language can facilitate your baby's speaking abilities, it can help him reach this major milestone as well. Many parents who have been signing with their children since they were infants say the use of ASL to assist in potty training proves effective because it allows your toddler to exhibit some control over processes in his life. Because your child received positive reinforcement for signing, the use of ASL — combined with the positivity surrounding potty training — can make the process less frustrating for all parties involved.

In many cases, your child may not be speaking at the time you begin to potty train. In this scenario, the sign for "potty" will help your child communicate with you that he needs to go to the bathroom. In fact, many parents say using sign language as a tool to facilitate potty training often allows your toddler to train faster, and with less frustration involved. In many cases, you will purchase a potty you can put in your bathroom, or simply a small seat that can be placed on top of your toilet. When your baby is ready to use the potty, you want to teach her the sign for "potty."

Using sign language to potty train is especially useful when a child is resistant to training or is not willing to train easily. Jennifer Simpson, a speech language pathologist and West Granby, Connecticut-based mother who taught her three children sign language, used ASL to facilitate potty training. She taught all of her children the sign for potty when they were approaching potty training, but found it to be most useful for her son. She says he was easily embarrassed if she asked him in public if he needed to go to the potty. Her son would always answer "no," even if he really had to go. She soon found that if she quietly got his attention and showed him the sign for "potty," he would agree to make that needed trip to the bathroom.

In addition to the sign for "potty," which would be your child's signal that he needs to use the bathroom, teach him the words for "toilet paper," "all done" (if you have not already taught this sign) "wash," "hands," and "good job." Use these signs as part of your potty training regimen. In fact, using them in sequence will help establish a routine that will be fun for your child and will make him eager to go on the potty.

If your child has already been using the sign for diaper change, continue to use this sign while potty training. If your child signs "diaper change," you may sign back "potty," and this becomes your opportunity to reinforce the need to use the potty.

Baby sign language potty training kits, which often include children's books, reward stickers, and a parent guide, are available on the market. Parents can use these kits to assist in potty training needs. However, by simply teaching your child the sign for "potty" and using it consistently, it will allow your child to express his need to use the bathroom in another way. Some parents report that initiating potty training at much earlier ages through the use of sign language helps children train before the age of 2, which is considered early by most parenting standards.

Situations and Solutions

Potty training is something that is individual for each child and parent. In fact, there is no right or wrong method to potty train your child. However, signing families may find themselves in several situations where signing can be used to facilitate the potty training process.

Situation No. 1: Your child has exhibited an interest in using the potty.

1. Show him the "potty" sign.

2. Tell him to make the sign when he needs to use the potty.

3. Any time he makes the sign, put him on the potty, even if he does not go to the bathroom.

4. If he is especially fond of the potty sign and is making it a dozen times a day, explain that he only needs to make it when he needs to go.

5. In the meantime, ask him to continue to use the "diaper change" sign.

6. When he makes the sign, you should say, "Next time, tell me when you have to go potty."

7. Make the "potty" sign when you say the word.

Situation No. 2: Your child is of potty training age (between 2 and 4 years old) and is resistant to using the potty.

1. Talk about how your child should use the potty and make the "potty" sign.

2. Tell your child you can put an end the use of diapers. Buy fun underwear with his favorite characters on them if — and only if — he decides to use the potty.

3. Have him sit in the potty every 30 to 45 minutes.

4. Every time you go to the potty, make the sign.

5. When he successfully uses the potty, offer some type of reward. This can be anything from a sticker to a few crackers.

Situation No. 3: Your child is starting to potty train but is having frequent accidents.

1. When your child has an accident, make the "potty" sign.

2. Say the words, "You need to go to the potty."

3. Put your child on the potty.

4. Repeat this every time he has an accident. Eventually, he will see the need to go to the potty before the accident occurs.

Situation No. 4: You are potty training, and your child is not wearing a diaper. You are in a public setting, such as a mall, a play date, or a party.

1. When you think it is the time when your child will need to use the potty, call his name and make the "potty" sign.

2. If he signs back "no," repeat the words and sign.

3. Once he complies, take him to the potty and make him sit down, even if he does not want to leave what he is doing.

Potty Training Timeline

The following is a three-month timeline for using sign language in your potty training routine.

Month No. 1: Introduce potty training to your child

Goal: Have your child learn the sign for potty.

Tools: A potty.

Exercise: Give your child a potty as a gift.

1. When he first gets the potty, he will be eager to sit on it.

2. Put it in the bathroom, and tell him it is a potty.

3. Make the sign for "potty."

4. Have him learn the sign though repetition. Use the sign when you yourself need to use the potty.

5. Say, "Mommy or Daddy needs to use the potty now," and make the sign for "potty."

6. Use the "potty" sign as much as possible for the first month.

7. If he does not begin to use the sign, show him it "hand-over-hand" so he knows how to make the sign.

Month No. 2: Reinforce the sign language

Goal: Have your child gain a better understanding of potty training through the use of sign language.

Tools: Books and DVDs about potty training.

Exercise: Once your child has learned the sign for "potty" — or is at least familiar with it — explain that he needs to recognize when he has to use the bathroom.

1. Read potty training storybooks to your child. Some good ones are: *The Potty Book For Girls* or *The Potty Book For Boys* (Barron's Educational Series, 2000), both by Alyssa Satin Capucilli and Dorothy Stott.

2. Each time the word "potty" is mentioned during the day, make the sign for "potty."

3. Integrate any other signs relating to bathroom use — including "toilet paper," "wash," "hands," and "towel" — that may be mentioned in the potty training book.

4. Read the book frequently to your child and continue to sign these words.

5. By the end of the month, your child should understand what he should do when he needs to use the potty.

Month No. 3: Make the sign language a habit

Goal: Have your child use sign language to tell you when he needs to use the potty.

Tools: Patience and new underwear for your child.

Exercise: Tell your child potty training has begun.

1. Plan to be at home or not out for long intervals of time. If your child attends daycare, make sure the teachers there know you are potty training. They may require he wear potty training pants to school.

2. Have your child say "bye bye" to diapers.

3. Give him a pair of underwear to wear with one of his favorite characters on them.

4. Begin to put him on the potty every 30 to 45 minutes and make the "potty" sign every time you do so. If your child is in daycare, ask that the teachers consistently continue this routine. In addition, you need to continue it at home.

Chapter Seven

ASL Connected to Learning Skills

I f you have decided to sign with your preverbal baby, it is likely your motivation has been to ignite early two-way communication with your child. However, as you delve deeper into this wonderful world of visual communication, you may find there are added benefits. In previous chapters, you have learned teaching your baby sign language can:

- Increase cognitive skills.

- Foster early verbal skills.

- Enhance interactions between you and your baby.

But will your little signer, who appeared to latch onto this visual language so remarkably easily, become advanced in her learning abilities due to her use of sign language? Many in the sign language community say this is so.

The first three years of your life are the most critical learning periods. A baby has millions of brain cells at this time, which will decrease with age. These early years are the most critical time to teach your child language development. Because your baby will be constantly fed information through this visual process, she will have a greater understanding of language, which will enhance her learning and reading skills.

Everything your child experiences affects her brain development. When you add sign language into her world, you are helping the millions of brain cells that she is born with multiply. These cells, called synapses, transmit knowledge to the brain. By using sign language, your child is forcing more connections in her brain that set the stage for enhanced learning.

When your child hears you speak words, her auditory skills are being formed. When there is a set of visual signs to match these words, she is stimulating the part of her brain that looks at things visually and kinesthetically. Now, she is not only hearing the word, but she is seeing the words and using touch to convey and understand the word. Because this learning comes in triplicate, her brain is working three times as hard than if it were just using her auditory skills.

Will My Baby Signer Become a Quick Reader?

In earlier chapters, you learned about Dr. Susan Goodwyn and Dr. Linda Acredolo's research, which revealed that babies who are taught to sign verbalized their wants and need earlier, and achieved higher IQ scores. In addition to their research, Dr. Joseph Garcia, who is known as a pioneer in the baby sign language industry, was among the first to reveal that babies who were taught sign language often had a better grasp of the English language than children who never learned to sign. Building on this research is the work of Marilyn Daniels who, in her book *Dancing With Words: Signing for Hearing Children's Literacy,* explains that continuing signing with your child once she can speak helps develop more of her brain's learning ability.

Daniels, through several documented studies, concluded that sign language can be used in hearing children to improve vocabulary and reading ability, among other learning abilities. In her 1991 studies, she gathered 14 hearing children who were taught ASL in preschool. They achieved higher scores — a collective mean score of 109.57 — on a picture vocabulary test than hearing children who were never taught to sign. The test, known as the Peabody Picture Vocabulary Test (PPVT), is a test published by American Guidance Company, which has been used since the 1960s. The test was revised in 1981 and is now called the PPVT-R. It caters to hearing people ages 6 months to 40 and is said to be well-respected and accurate. Standard testing scores have a mean of 100 and a standard deviation of 15, reports Daniels in her book. She cites the 109.57 mean score as a "powerful number that clearly indicates that children who learned ASL as preschoolers acquired a larger English vocabulary than is expected of typical children."

The tests that measure the recognition of vocabulary words are the first steps in teaching a child to read. In typical learning environments, children usually start learning "sight words" in kindergarten. These words, which start with easy two- and three-letter words, such as "an," "the" and "but," progress throughout the year to more difficult words that are used to form sentences. Once children have a large range of vocabulary words that they can recognize by sight, they are on their way to reading. Children who use ASL to communicate have been shown to have more advanced vocabulary recognition, which often leads to early reading skills.

Another of Daniels' studies, conducted in 1994, tested and tracked hearing students from their first weeks as prekindergarten students until their last weeks as kindergarten students. For the first year, they received sign language instruction, but not in the second year in the kindergarten classroom setting. However, the students' mean score on the standardized English vocabulary test jumped from 77.84 (before kindergarten) to 95.11 (after kindergarten). The results revealed that the children made "statistically significant vocabulary gains" during prekindergarten, which carried over into kindergarten. Her findings serve as a reason to include sign language in early childhood curriculum to enhance early vocabulary recognition skills, which fosters reading skills in preschool-age children.

Did You Know?

"If you look at a brain scan of young people who have been exposed to gestural communication, there are different hot spots and stimulations going on. What you are stimulating with sign language is fine motor muscle. The vocal cords are fine motor muscles, and you have a symbiotic relationship going on."

— Dawn Babb Prochovnic, founder of SmallTalk Learning

While there are many schools of thought as to why signing babies tend to be quicker learners, it could be due to the fact that signing parents are those who are more intent on teaching their children than those parents who see that duty solely as the responsibility of a child's teacher. The signing parent is one who is very conscious of enhancing his or her child's ability to learn, grow, and communicate. For this reason, many in the sign language community say these parents will likely raise children who are more eager to learn, and in many cases, this eagerness translates into quicker learners. Sign language, because it is visual, helps your child think visually very early on in life. For this reason, these children tend to grasp concepts in visual terms.

Early Signers Equal Early Spellers

Fingerspelling words in sign language have been found to greatly aid in your child's early spelling abilities. Early signers who use fingerspelling will learn how to spell words easier and faster, as they recognize each visual sign for the letters and have already gotten in the habit of spelling words. For example, if your child learns the word "cat" as one of her first words, you will show her the written word for "cat."

If she has learned the sign language alphabet, she will likely learn how to spell this word in sign language before she has developed the fine motor skills to write it on paper. The fine motor skills needed to write and print letters will take longer to develop in your child than her ability to finger-spell words. Because of this, sign language can help your child become an early speller and, therefore, read earlier than her peers. In fact, studies have shown that children can better memorize the spelling of words if they have been taught to spell through fingerspelling.

In many cases, children who have learned how to fingerspell words will use it to help them remember how to spell words. They have the visual sign language images to picture in their minds as they sound out the words. According to Marilyn Daniels, the signs used in ASL serve as pictures for your child to visualize when they are learning the meaning of words. Therefore, when learning to spell and read, your child will reveal the sign for the word being learned, and this will serve as a visual sign or recognition for her. The signing child can think more clearly and uses sign language as a recognition tool for early spelling abilities.

If you taught your preverbal baby sign language and continued to use it as she develops her speech, it is likely that she will be a visual learner. Use the following sign language exercises to simulate her visual learning skills:

Exercise No. 1

1. Pick your child's favorite song, and instead of simply signing the words in the song, take a pen and paper and write down key words as you both listen to the song play on a CD player or on an mp3 player dock.

2. Once you have a list of at least ten words, begin to fingerspell the words.

3. At first, your child — especially if spelling is not yet a skill she has developed — will need to look at each letter, recognize the letter in the word, then remember the sign. Your child is learning to recognize letters, put them together to make words, and then translate that word into sign language.

Exercise No. 2

1. Choose a word that is visual, such as "flower."

2. Say the word and make a gesture, such as if you are sniffing a flower.

3. Illustrate the sign for "flower."

4. Next, also fingerspell the word. Make the sign for the letter "F," and depending on your child's spelling abilities, continue with the signs for each letter of the word.

Exercise No. 3

1. Tell your child to say the first word that comes to her mind when you say a word.

2. For example, say "hot."

3. Make the sign for "hot."

4. She may say the word "cold."

5. Ask her to respond by also making the sign for "cold."

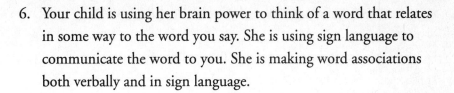

6. Your child is using her brain power to think of a word that relates in some way to the word you say. She is using sign language to communicate the word to you. She is making word associations both verbally and in sign language.

Exercise No. 4

1. Fill a box with random items, for example, a lemon, orange, doll, two books, and a pair of slippers.

2. Ask your child to close her eyes, reach in the box, and pull out an item with her eyes still closed.

3. Ask her to guess what the item is simply by touch and ask her to say the word for the item.

4. Once she says the word, tell her to put the item back in the box, then have her open her eyes.

5. Now, face her and make eye contact. Ask her to make the sign for the word for the item. This game allows your child use her sense of touch to initiate her visual skills to identify the "mystery item."

Exercise No. 5

1. Cut out pictures from magazines.

2. Take regular writing paper and write the word for each item or person pictured on a separate piece of paper.

3. Put the written words and pictures in different boxes or hats.

4. Let your child pick out a word from the hat without looking inside.

5. Open the paper and read the word to your child.

6. Ask her to find the picture that goes with the word.

7. Tell her to make the sign for the written word and picture she has chosen.

It is not just fingerspelling that boosts your child's learning ability. Any time she uses her hands to form signs, it is forcing her to do something while learning what a word means or sounds like. In addition to making her think in visual terms, it forces her to kinesthetically learn. She is combining auditory learning with visual learning.

When your child uses sign language, she is making more brain connections. Her brain is seeing the sign, processing it and, in a sense, translating it into the English word for the sign. Every time your child sees a sign, then another brain connection, so to speak, is made. You child is becoming smarter each time she learns something new, and sign language promotes this type of learning.

A big part of your child's early development via sign language is dependent on you. If you encourage signing and show you understand the signs she is making, you are acknowledging her early attempts at signing, and you will foster a visual learner. Because it takes a while to master signs, your child will be used to trial and error as part of her early learning skills.

CASE STUDY: KRISTEN BURRIS

1473 N Watson Way
Eagle, Idaho 83616
(208) 938-1277
Eaglekristen@gmail.com

Kristen Burris began learning sign language in sixth grade. She started signing with her first son, Jackson, when he was 4 months old to help calm his tantrums that stemmed from colic. She found that soon after he learned to sign, his colic had resolved. She also signed with her second son, Colton, since he was 8 months old.

My son was able to communicate thoughts, needs, and wants before he could speak. It was incredible. Both sons learned how to sign "sleepy," which is a mother's dream come true. Colton often walks by my cutting board where I prepare his bottles. Out of nowhere, he will sign "milk," and he will drink an entire bottle. If he did not know sign language I probably would have never figured out what he needed at that time.

When Jackson was 1 year old, we were at the beach and an airplane flew overhead — and he signed "airplane." It was so exciting. Colton was 14 months old and signed "dog" when he heard the neighbor's dog barking. It still seems to be his favorite and most consistent sign.

Signing also reduced whining and screaming at a young age. When around other children the same age who could not sign, they would whine and whimper until their mothers figured out what they were trying to communicate. Often times, it was excruciating to hear and watch. It was quite deflating to finally realize the child just wanted a sip of water or something simple.

The benefits of signing made me feel empowered that was I contributing to the best cognitive and loving start for my boys. It touches my heart so deeply when my boys sign "I love you." Those are memories that last a lifetime. I have been so moved by getting feedback from my babies at such a young age without just crying as a form of communication. I also look forward to meeting deaf people in the future so all of us can converse in ways most people cannot with them.

Our children are exceptionally bright. Doctors, teachers, child psychologists, nannies, and friends all comment on how advanced they are and how proficient my 3-year-old's vocabulary is. One of our nannies, who has three boys of her own, said she thinks Jackson is borderline genius because by 2 years old, he knew his entire alphabet by signing. He also knows all of the sounds to every letter. He can count to 10 and is very inquisitive about how everything works. If you give him the opportunity, he will tell you how our coffee maker works, how gas goes in our car, or how the washer and dryer function. The little man never stops talking.

My older son is teaching our baby now, and it is a lot of fun. When I feed them something yummy, they almost always excitedly sign "more!" My children use sign language to observe the world around them. Spontaneously, my 18-month-old will sign "dog," "I love you," or "sleepy." His most used sign is "all done" as he throws his hands into the air after a meal.

I feel the bond is stronger with my children because they know I understand them at a very early age. I am not guessing — I am communicating, and that gives them confidence to know I will always be there to help them in this world. I also feel it has given me another tool to express concern for them.

Facilitate Learning Through ASL

In the same way you used sign language to communicate with your baby, use ASL to continue to teach your child. As she discovers her words, she will ask you the names for objects in her world. For example, your 3 year old might ask what the big red sign says as you stop the car at an intersection. You can tell her it is a "stop sign," and make the sign for "stop" and "sign," and explain to her why cars have to come to a halt when they encounter these signs. Your child is now learning more signs. She is learning about her world, and she is learning the meaning of words in English as well as in ASL. Do this for all the curious questions that come up. As your child learns about her world, she will better understand and be in tune with it as she continues her signs language journey.

CASE STUDY: HEATHER M. KENDEL

Interpreter, Director, ASL Advocates
494 East 200th Street
Euclid, Ohio 44119
216-862-2978 or 216-240-2704
jeak1027@aol.com

Heather M. Kendel learned the ASL alphabet from a friend when she was 10 years old. After teaching all four of her children sign language, she decided to found an organization based on ASL. She is the founder of ASL Advocates, which is an organization that facilitates effective and respectful communication among the deaf, deaf-blind, hard-of-hearing, and hearing communities alike. The organization also promotes independence, tolerance, and human rights for all. The organization offers English as a second language (ESL) tutoring, food banks, mentoring, and social work services.

Babies are trying to learn eye coordination, which takes time, but this helps develop that skill much quicker. I have learned that babies who sign usually talk sooner than those who do not. Babies learn that signs represent things, and the more they learn, the more they want to know. It is fascinating to watch. I see that parents are less frustrated and calmer when using sign language.

Babies and young children learn to communicate with the basics. School-age children whom we work with learn that it is all right if a sign is not perfect and that there are no wrong questions. They learn there is no reason to be afraid to express themselves. Children learn at ASL Advocates that talking with their hands is something many in this country do, whether deaf or not. They learn about deaf pride. Teenagers grasp the concepts better and know that this is in fact another language. Most go on to take more classes.

One of the most awesome things I was able to see from a child taking my class is that he was able to surpass his parents. Although his parents did a wonderful job, the child has an insatiable need to learn more. I see that he practices and, each week, never falters in remembering the lessons of past weeks. He helps his parents continue to learn as well. He clearly defines what he wants or needs through signs, and the temper tantrums that once prevailed are no longer because he can communicate clearly. Because we work with the deaf, they are active in helping with classes so that individuals, regardless of age, have full exposure to the deaf community and its culture, not just the language.

I started signing with all of my children within hours of their birth. My children are James, 16, Eileen, 15, Abigeal, 11, and Kathleen, 10. I loved using sign language because I knew that I had a bond with my children that no one else would. My son, James, uses it in school to try to communicate with other deaf students, as well as the interpreters who are readily available in his "special ed" program. He is autistic, has severe ADHD, and is multiple handicapped. My daughter Eileen now uses it to this day and works as the youth director at the organization. I have used it with my two other children as well. My daughter Abigeal was speaking in full sentences before she was 1 year old. It helped my children communicate; it helps me when they are misbehaving in public. I sign to them to stop it or settle down, and they usually do. I feel that it also helped with their speech and language skills.

My daughter used to have many tantrums, and ASL helped for several reasons. Watching the signing gave her reason to focus on something else. She knew that she got what she asked for, such as a drink or food, so that helped. All my children look at words as pictures, so it helps them grasp concepts more easily. They definitely had an easier time when it came to speaking, and they began to reach for things at an earlier age. Their hand-eye coordination developed quicker as well.

Chapter Eight

Troubleshooting — Solving Common Sign Language Problems

With anything you will teach your child — to talk, read, walk, or sign — there will be mistakes, mishaps, and malfunctions. Teaching sign language to your child is not any different. In fact, there are many problems that may arise during the process of learning sign language. For example, if your child has been exposed to sign language since he was 6 months old, he is accustomed to this visual communication and has begun to use it. However, once he becomes focused on a new task at hand, such as learning to crawl, he may drop signing because he is now using his hands to get places and has less time to look directly at you and sign his needs to you. This chapter will identify sign language problems and illustrate ways to correctly troubleshoot them.

Do Not Make Signing a Chore

As mentioned in previous chapters, if signing is not something your child looks upon favorably, it will not be something he will have the urge to do. Continue playing games that you can integrate sign language into, and use the lesson plans listed in Chapter 4 to continue to teach your child to use sign language. By using the lesson plans, you will keep signing fun and initiate your child's continued use of this visual language. Often, one of the biggest reasons for the lack of signing will be that your child has either grown bored with signing or looks at it as an extra chore.

Overzealous parents may find they become too concerned with teaching their baby sign language and may lose track of why it is being taught in the first place. If you were teaching your child to also speak French, you would not be teaching him complex words and phrases at the start. You would take it slowly and teach the French words that he would understand the meaning of first. Similarly, this is how you should seek to teach your child sign language. Keep in mind that your child, when he attends school, may learn some signs on his own.

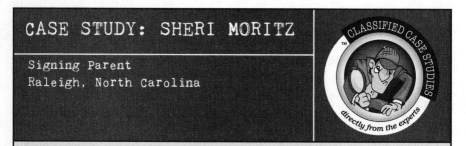

CASE STUDY: SHERI MORITZ

Signing Parent
Raleigh, North Carolina

Sheri Moritz only knew a very small amount of sign language. She had experience with sign language as a teenager because her friend had an aunt with Down syndrome who used sign language to communicate with her family. Moritz saw their ability to communicate with her using sign language and wanted to know more about this visual language. A psychology major with a concentration in child development, she read studies that found children could communicate at an earlier age with the use of sign language, so she used sign language with her daughter, Morgan.

I started signing with Morgan, who is currently 2 years old, when she was about 3 months old. We bought the Baby Einstein signing video. While she sat in her swing, she would watch the video over and over again. It seemed to be the easiest way for me to introduce it to her when she could not even hold up her head, let alone sign.

Morgan's first signing words were "eat," "bath," and "play" when she was about 12 months old. She used them constantly when wanting to communicate those three things. She mostly used sign language to convey a want. We knew when she was hungry, which made things so much easier.

Signing was an amazing enhancement to our communication. There seemed to be less frustration from the adults who could figure out if she was sleepy, hungry, or bored. She has just recently started speaking, but we still use sign language in addition to spoken words to communicate.

Instead of tantrums, we dealt with having to tell her "no" when we knew what Morgan wanted because she could sign it. Signing allowed her to understand what we were asking her to do, as well. It helped with hand-eye coordination, as well as her ability to associate an activity or item with a word. With an increased ability to communicate, we were able to focus on the task or desire without having to figure out what she wanted or simply ignoring her, assuming she was mumbling.

There is a child with Down syndrome in her daycare class, so the teachers had also implemented sign language in the classroom. All of the children were able to communicate by the age of 12 to 18 months before any of them could speak.

Morgan progressed fairly rapidly in her ability to sign. I think that was because we had a high focus on it. We constantly used sign language with her at home, and she also used it at daycare. The largest problem we ran into was that a couple of the parents at the daycare did not want their children learning sign language because they thought it would delay their child's speech. When the daycare had to eliminate signing, we continued it at home. We also had many people in public who thought Morgan was hearing impaired because we would sign in public. In those situations, I would explain that we were trying to teach her to communicate quicker, and then they often thought it was neat. They would inquire as to how well it worked.

Her speech is much more comprehensible than the other children in her class. Although she is the youngest in her class, she is always the first to move up because she is able to communicate. She has a lot of word and picture recognition as well.

Common Sign Language Problems and Solutions

Like any other learned skill, sign language will have its problems. In some cases, it may be a problem you are experiencing in your continued effort to teach your child sign language, and in other circumstances it may be mishaps, such as your child making the wrong sign or using the same sign for a multitude of words. But for every problem there is a logical solution that will help you overcome the hurdle at hand.

Following is a list of 20 common problems that may arise when teaching sign language to your child, and ways to troubleshoot each problem. The most important thing is for parents to recognize the signing obstacle and implement the right solution that will help continue your child's interest in sign language.

Problem: Your child makes the same sign for everything

Why this happens: Your child mastered a sign, and he uses it for everything from wanting milk to needing a diaper change. This might be happening because this was your child's first sign and he mastered it. You rewarded him for making the sign, and he feels proud. You can see that he likes to use sign language, but for some reason he really likes making this particular sign. It is no different from a child who learns the word "Mommy" and uses it to get the attention of not only his mother but also his father, aunt, uncle, and grandparents when he wants them.

Solution: Continue to model signs consistently throughout your day. If you say the word "more," clearly enunciate it and make sure you are in your child's view when making the sign. By watching you over and over again, your child will learn more signs and will eventually add them to his signing repertoire.

Problem: You misunderstand your baby's signs

Why this happens: Several signs have similar movements or gestures. For this reason, it is easy to mistake the sign your child might be making for "ball" when he really is signing that he is hurt (both signs have movements that are performed near the waist).

Solution: Watch your child's signs carefully. If he looks as if he is about to cry, you might initially think he is hurt in some way and are expecting him to sign the word "hurt." But be sure to notice the subtle cues and nuances in your child's sign language, and watch where his gaze is focused. You might think he is hurt, but he may be looking at the ball that just rolled under a car and out of your view. He may be signing the word for "ball," and he may look sad because she thinks he lost it and wants you to get it.

Problem: You fail to sign because your hands are full

Why this happens: Before your baby begins to walk, he is reliant on you for transportation. In many cases, you are carrying him up and down the stairs, to and from the car, and from room to room.

Solution: Shift your baby into one arm to make your sign. Even a two-handed sign can be performed with one hand. For example, the sign for "more" is done by putting your two hands together with the fingertips meeting in the middle in front of your body. If you have your child in your arms, you can make the sign for "more" with one hand meeting the air or meeting up against your baby's body.

Problem: Your baby drops sign language once he can talk

Why this happens: He can now tell you what he wants, so he does not see the need to continue to use sign language to communicate with you.

Solution: Continue signing to him. Use every opportunity to integrate sign language into your day. Sign key words during meals, play, bath, and at bedtime. It is very important to use sign language during playtime, so he sees it as fun. It is all right to make signing part of fun and games in order to continue your baby's interest in using it to communicate with you.

Problem: Your child confuses signs

Why this happens: Your baby may initially confuse signs while getting the hang of using sign language. He may confuse more abstract signs that have no relation between the words and how the signs are performed. He may sign "milk" when he meant to sign "more." He may sign "cat" when he meant to sign "dog." And he may sign "diaper change" when he meant to sign "potty." The reason is he simply got confused. This is a similar situation as when you may get tongue-tied and use the wrong word while multi-tasking, or you call someone by the wrong name.

Solution: If your child signs "milk" when he obviously wants more of the banana you are feeding him, ask, "Do you want more banana?" Make the sign for "more "and for "banana." By showing him the correct signs over and over, he will eventually begin to use the correct sign when he wants the item in question.

Problem: Your child does not make the signs the proper way

Why this happens: This is known as sign approximation and is very common in early signers. In fact, many babies will make the signs to their best abilities. Your child has small hands, so he may not have the fine motor skills to make every sign perfectly, especially when signs require the use of both hands.

Solution: Continue to correctly model the signs. Make sure that you are in your child's view when you make the sign, and that he can see you clearly when you make it. Also, be sure to speak the words for the signs to reinforce the meaning. Just like your child will use baby talk with words like "ba ba" for bottle, his signs will be tend to be shortened versions of the correct way to perform a sign. Just like his speech evolves in time because you are speaking the words correctly to him, his signs will become more precise as you continue to model them for him.

Problem: Your child refuses to make basic need or feeling signs

Why this happens: Your child may need to see an object to be able to make the sign. This is due to his need for the visual image to connect to the sign. Though he may enjoy making the sign for "duck" and "milk" every time he sees his bottle or a rubber ducky that accompanies him in the bathtub, he does not have anything to support visual recognition for the sign "hungry" or "thirsty."

Solution: Continue to make these signs even though your child does not use them. He may not have developed the need to make the sign in his daily life just yet. Once he does this and has seen the sign made by you many times in the proper context, it is more likely he will mimic it. To solve this issue, it is important to also use signs in different situations. For example, show him the sign for "eat" during breakfast. Later, during play time, say, "Let's feed your toy bear." Make sign for "eat" when you pretend to feed his favorite toy bear.

Problem: Signing turns into a power struggle

Why this happens: You want your baby to sign and are getting frustrated that he will not do it. The baby may try to communicate without signing. You might tell him, "Please make the sign for [the item he wants] in order to get it."

Solution: Do not force your child to sign. He has to do it in his own time and when it is most comfortable for him. If you force using ASL, it may not come.

Problem: Your child makes signs on the wrong part of the body

Why this happens: Because your child is just learning to sign, he may not know where a sign should be made, and often the location of the sign can change its meaning. For example, he may make the sign for "Mom" on his lips instead of his chin, and it may look more like the sign for "eat."

Solution: Model the sign correctly and explain how and where it should be done. For example, say, "Touch your throat when you make the sign for 'thirsty.'"

Problem: Your baby makes up her own signs

Why this happens: If your baby does not know the sign for a word, she may try her own "homemade" sign.

Solution: Many sign language experts say homemade signs or gestures are all right if the parent understands what the child is trying to say. However, if you want to groom a bilingual child, it is best to continue to model the sign correctly so the child will continue to use it in the future.

Problem: Your child is not progressing in her sign language skills

Why this happens: Your child gets to a point where she knows about a dozen signs that she uses and refuses to learn more signs. This can be for two reasons:

- She may not see the need to use the new signs you are showing her.

- You are not showing her signs that are relevant to her world.

Solution: You need to show signs that she will find important to her life. Besides favorite foods and games, show her the signs for objects she uses regularly, such as "toothbrush," "toothpaste," "brush," "comb," "shirt," and "pants." Continue using signs when you say these words, and make sure to say the words.

Problem: Your child is not focusing on sign language

Why this happens: Your child, as he grows, is discovering many new and fun things in his world. From learning how to run and jump, to discovering that ice cream is cold, his entire world is about new things. He may stop signing when he is reaching a new milestone, such as crawling or walking. In this case, he is busy with the task at hand, rather than using sign language.

Solution: Make signing continuously fun and new by integrating new signs and using the signs he already knows in fun ways. For example, if you go pumpkin picking in the fall, then as you and your child roam through the pumpkin patch, ask him to say and sign what he sees. This is a new place to use signing with him, and it is fun.

Problem: Your child is reluctant to sign in sentences

Why this happens: Your child may enjoy making one-word signs that accompany his speech once he begins to talk and refuses to expand his signing to two-word phrases and sentences. For example, he may not see the need to sign "dog" and "walk," but when he signs "dog" after lunch, he is telling you he wants to come with you on your daily walk with the dog.

Solution: Pretend you do not understand. If you have begun to understand that your child's one-word signs take on the meaning of a whole sentence, then try to coax your child into signing more words of the sentence. If he signs "dog," ask, "What would you like to do with the dog?"

Problem: Your child starts to use sign language in place of speech once he can talk

Why this happens: If your child would rather sign than say words to you throughout your day, he may have become too reliant on sign language as his mode of communication.

Solution: If you want your child to both sign and speak to you when he makes a sign, ask him questions that will force speech. For example, if you tell him to clean his room, and he signs "no," ask why he will not clean his room. He is more likely to speak "Because I do not want to" than sign that sentence.

Problem: You cannot find the time to continue signing

Why this happens: You have had a second child or have gone back to work. Because your child can talk, the need for communication via sign language no longer exists.

Solution: Make a conscious effort to continue signing with your child, even if you do not learn new signs yourself or teach them to your child. Make an effort to at least make five signs a day. Remember, the more you sign with your child, the greater the likelihood that he will become bilingual with sign language as his second language.

Problem: Your child signs to other people who do not understand sign language

Why this happens: Because signing becomes natural to your child, he may try to sign to his grandparents, neighbors, or early childhood friends. If they do not know sign language, they are confused by these gestures.

Solution: Teach the caregivers in his life. *See the next chapter, Chapter 9, on the importance of the babysitter or nanny knowing sign language.* Show them key signs that your child uses every day. These could be the basic need and feeling signs, or simply the signs for your child's favorite foods. This will allow participating adults to also communicate with your child via sign language. You may, however, need to explain to your child that his friend next door does not know sign language, but maybe the friend could be taught a few words.

Problem: Members of your family do not accept sign language

Why this happens: People who do not know about the benefits of teaching your preverbal baby to sign may not be on board with your signing repertoire. This person could be your mother, mother-in-law, or best friend.

Solution: Explain to this person that signing has helped you form a stronger bond with your child and allowed him to communicate early needs to you before he could speak. Also, tell this person to read this book to learn all the benefits of signing with your child. If the person chooses not to partake in signing with your child, explain that your child may not always understand if the person chooses to communicate this way.

Problem: You cannot keep up with all the signs your baby wants to learn

Why this happens: Your child may be a quick learner and has developed a thirst for leaning more signs. If he can talk, he may ask you how to make new signs all day.

Solution: If you are not proficient in ASL, keep this book handy. When your child asks you how to make a sign, take a few moments to look it up and teach it to him. If you are in the middle of something important and cannot look it up at that particular time, tell him you promise to look it up later and teach it to him. Be sure to keep your promise.

Problem: Your child will not sign in public

Why this happens: Though he will sign to you all day at home, once you set foot into a public arena, your child stops signing. Because he sees that this is not the main form of communication outside your home, he might choose to drop the signing in places where people do not understand it, or he may be embarrassed or afraid to do it outside the home.

Solution: Do not force your child to use sign language in public. Encourage it by using it yourself, but allow him to choose when and if he used it outside the home. As he grows more proficient in his sign language skills, he will likely use it more regularly, which will include when you are in a place other than the home.

Problem: Your child is learning sign language faster than you

Why this happens: You likely chose to learn sign language along with your child. But although he can spend his days learning new signs from DVDs, school, or daycare, you may be preoccupied with all of life's other duties.

Solution: Let him teach you what he has learned in these other situations. Do not worry about this role reversal. If your child is comfortable enough showing you a new sign, simply as him what that sign is and learn from him.

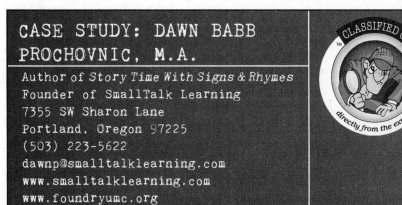

CASE STUDY: DAWN BABB
PROCHOVNIC, M.A.

Author of *Story Time With Signs & Rhymes*
Founder of SmallTalk Learning
7355 SW Sharon Lane
Portland, Oregon 97225
(503) 223-5622
dawnp@smalltalklearning.com
www.smalltalklearning.com
www.foundryumc.org

Dawn Babb Prochovnic's interest in sign language was ignited at a young age. She currently teaches a variety of different signing workshop formats customized for all ages in libraries, schools, child care centers, community centers, and hospitals/birthing centers. She also teaches in private homes and workplaces under the business name SmallTalk Learning. She is also a children's author and has written eight picture books related to signing, titled Story Time With Signs & Rhymes. *These books explore early childhood concepts such as colors, animals, and "things that go" through lyrical language and ASL.*

When my first child, Katia, was born in 1999, signing became an important part of her early communication. Katia was the child who not only wanted a cup of water, but she wanted it "in the red cup, please." Signing made it possible for her to tell us what she was thinking and what she needed before she was able to clearly communicate verbally. Signing went from being something that our family started doing just for fun to being a critical part of surviving the preverbal stages of development with a bright, communicative, spirited child. Back then, signing was more of an "alternative" thing to do — it was definitely not mainstream.

Through sign language, children can communicate their preferences, such as being hungry for a banana or a cracker, or being thirsty for water or milk. My favorite part about signing with babies is that it empowers them to initiate con versations with you about things that are important to them, which you may otherwise never become aware of. These early conversations provide the foundation for a deep and lasting communication relationship with your child. There is also a growing body of research that shows that early exposure to sign language contributes to early literacy benefits.

Babies who sign from an early age have also been shown to talk sooner than babies who do not sign. This also helps develop broader vocabularies sooner.

Children who take my classes learn that signing will help them be better readers and stronger spellers. It is fun to do; it will give them something to do with their busy hands; it is like a code to unlock; and it will help them communicate with people who are deaf.

Although it is true there are benchmarks that pediatricians and other professionals use for assessing whether a child is progressing on a normal trajectory related to verbal acquisition, most parents do not talk with their babies with these benchmarks in mind as a goal. Parents do not typically set verbal achievement goals for their babies when they verbally interact with them. Parents read, sing, and talk to their babies. All the while, babies giggle, coo, kick their feet, and wave their arms to show they are engaged in the "conversation." Parents trust and fully expect that their babies will gradually start verbalizing back to them in their own time.

Parents are pretty relaxed about the way they teach their babies to point and wave. I find that parents are more successful with signing if they are equally relaxed in the way they teach their babies to sign.

Chapter Nine

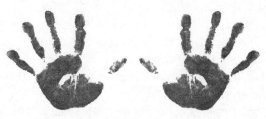

Should My Babysitter or Nanny Also Use Sign Language?

If you and your spouse are using sign language to communicate with your child, she will likely start using signs to "talk" back with you. However, your child will not recognize that this is just something she does with Mommy and Daddy. In fact, she will likely use sign language to tell Grandma that she loves her, the nanny that she wants more applesauce, and the store clerk that she likes toys.

If your child spends a considerable amount of time with a nanny or babysitter, she will want to use sign language to communicate with this person. In fact, if this person does not understand your child's signs, it is likely that she will stop signing. For this reason, the nanny or babysitter needs to be part of your sign language regime.

Did You Know?

"If my baby knows the signs for 'more,' 'milk,' and 'diaper change,' and now I drop my baby off with someone who does not speak sign language, that is grounds for frustration. If my baby says 'ba ba' when she wants her special blanket, the daycare provider will be interested in knowing that is what she wants when she says those words. If your nanny is not interested in sign language, I would be worried about what else she is not interested in."

— Dawn Babb Prochovnic, founder of SmallTalk Learning

Making Sign Language Part of Your Household

Once you have made sign language part of your household where all the members of the family use some sign language to aid in verbal language or to communicate with a preverbal baby or hearing-impaired child, it is time to bring the extended family into the fold. It may start with simply teaching Grandpa how to sign "I love you," or an aunt how to say "more milk." Those extended family members should be able to understand your child's signs when she makes them.

Previous chapters have included ways to make signing part of your daily activities. When you have family or friends over, the signs that are part of your daily routine do not have to cease. In fact, if you continue to use sign language with your child, it will often end up being the topic of conversation when you are with family and friends — especially if you have a preverbal baby who signs. In many cases, once your family or friends have witnessed your child ask for more cereal via sign language, they will want to join in on this communication with your child. Offer to teach extended family members or friends who frequent your household any words they would like to learn in sign language. It only takes a few seconds to illustrate a sign, and now you have another person communicating with your child through sign language.

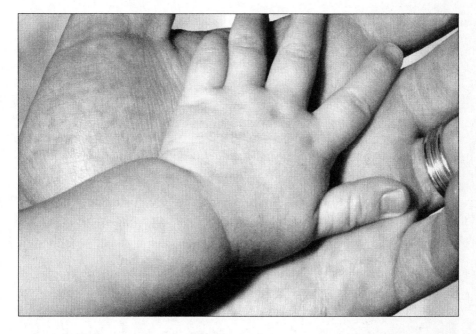

Why Should I Have Other Caregivers Sign with My Child?

If you are signing at home, it is imperative that other caregivers understand your child's means of communication. If your daughter makes the sign for "more" after she eats her applesauce for lunch and your nanny does not understand her sign, your child will likely get frustrated that she is not being understood. A tantrum or bout of crying may follow. For this reason, you must teach your nanny sign language.

If you obtained your nanny through an agency, sign language may very well have been part of his or her training. If this is the case, the nanny may not only continue what you have taught your child, but foster the teaching aspects of how to sign with your child as well. However, you do not want your nanny to teach your child signs that you do not know. For this reason, you need good communication between yourself and your nanny about what is being taught to your child and what she is learning.

If the nanny does not know any sign language, you must take the time before you go to work to teach the nanny signs your child has learned. For example, if you have introduced the signs for "more," "milk," "happy" and "sad" over the weekend, then on Monday morning you will need your nanny to arrive 20 minutes early. In this time, you can show him or her the signs, as a well as provide the nanny with some illustrations about how to make to the sign. It would be helpful if you provide the nanny with this book so he or she can look up any signs she may forget. You will need to instruct the nanny to use it as frequently as possible during her time spent with your child. Your nanny should be doing everything that you do in your sign language regimen.

If your child attends daycare, some sign language may be taught, especially if there are deaf or other special-needs children in the class. However, you should make it known to the daycare center that you are using sign language to communicate with your child. Once your child starts signing, she will try to communicate with daycare center providers in this way. You can do the same thing with a daycare center teacher that you would do with the non-signing nanny. Arrive 20 minutes early to drop your child off and show the teacher the signs your child is using. Although the daycare provider may not be able to use as many signs in a one-on-one situation, he or she at least understands the signs your child is making so he or she will best attend to your child's needs.

If your nanny is more fluent in sign language than you are, then you may want take 20 minutes with her when you arrive home in order to learn the signs that she may have taught your child during the day. Even if she simply writes you a list of the signs, you can look them up on a Web site or in the sign language dictionary at the end of this book, and continue to use them with your child after the nanny has introduced them to him.

When Other Caregivers do not Understand Your Baby's Signs

When other caregivers do not understand your baby's signs, there is a barrier to communication that can inhibit the process of your child's development of sign language. If she only signs with you, her chances of becoming bilingual are also inhibited. Many parents will ask, "Even if I show my caregiver sign language, how will I know she is using it throughout the day as much as I would like her to?" If the nanny is a trusted caregiver, and you emphasize the importance of his or her use of sign language with your child, then he or she will likely do as instructed. The working parent has an extra task of teaching the nanny sign language in this instance.

In some respects, teaching another adult who is eager to learn is easier than teaching a child. The most important aspect of this process is not only showing the nanny signs, but fully explaining to him or her how to teach them to your child. Again, this book would prove to be a useful resource to the nanny who will need to know when, where, how, and why signing with your child is beneficial.

Did You Know?

"If you are really serious about your child learning sign language, the more people who are doing it with them in their world, the more likely they are to use it."

— Barbara Desmarais, a Canada-based parenting and life coach who teaches sign language to babies

Importance of Reinforcement From Other Caregivers

If the person who cares for your child is continuing to teach your son signs and carry on your signing routine, it is more likely your child will view this as a second language and will use it to communicate. Similarly, if one parent works part-time and you leave your child with relatives or a babysitter for periods of time during the week, it is just as important for these caregivers to use sign language for your child. Your child needs to be understood at all times, especially when she is first learning how to sign.

Because of the bonding between parent and child through sign language, some parents are hesitant to teach their child sign language because they fear the child will bond closer to the nanny through the use of ASL. But though the nanny may grow close to the child through sign language, as long as you are using it as well for bonding in your own way, it is highly doubtful that sign language will bring the nanny closer to the child than you.

Tips for teaching the babysitter or nanny sign language

In the same way that you have taught your baby sign language, you must now teach the nanny who will care for her as well. Do not think of this as an arduous task. In fact, it will be fun and very different from teaching your child. Teaching an adult who can grasp concepts easier that a child should be easy. If your nanny is eager, or at least willing, to learn sign language to communicate with your child, you will be successful in your teaching of sign language to him or her.

Follow these exercises for teaching the nanny sign language and how to use it with your child:

Exercise No. 1

1. Ask the nanny to recap his or her day with your child.

2. As you listen to their activities, think of five signs that would be relevant to their routine.

3. Write down the five signs and show the nanny how to make the signs.

4. Ask him or her to make the signs with you and to practice them throughout the day.

Exercise No. 2

1. Ask the nanny to come up with five words he or she thinks your child would use if he could speak.

2. Tell the nanny to write them on paper for you.

3. Show the nanny the signs for each word at your next meeting.

4. Ask him or her to do the signs with you.

Exercise No. 3

1. Test your nanny on the learned skills. Ask her when he or she is using the signs he or she has learned.

2. Ask the nanny to show you how and when he or she makes the signs with your child.

3. Ask the nanny to log your child's progress by writing down in a journal all the signs your child attempts or completes.

Chapter Ten

Signing to Deaf and Hard-of-Hearing Children

W hen a baby is born in a hospital, the pediatrician will evaluate the infant for various physical abilities. In this evaluation, the doctor will look for signs that the baby can hear. Referred to as the Newborn Hearing Screening Test, this examination will tell a doctor if your child can hear correctly. If it is found that she cannot hear as she should, further testing can be done. Hard-of-hearing individuals can hear some sound, while deaf individuals cannot hear anything.

Did You Know?

Out of every 1,000 children born in the United States, about three are deaf or hard-of-hearing. Out of every ten children born deaf, about nine are born to hearing parents. Approximately 15 percent (26 million) Americans between the ages of 20 and 69 have high frequency hearing loss due to exposure to loud sounds or noise at work or in leisure activities.

— The National Institute on Deafness and Other Communication Disorders

When a hearing issue is detected in an infant, it can be determined how much or how little your child can hear. A test called a behavioral audiogram can be used to detect the quietest sound a child can hear. Often, these tests are for the older child who can elicit a response, such as raising a hand when a sound is heard. There are, however, tests for babies. These are known as electro-physiological tests, which can be given to a child who has yet to develop fine motor skills to generate a physical response to sound.

There are two types of electro-physiological tests that can be administered to newborns:

Auditory brainstem responses (ABR): This procedure calls for sensors to be placed on a baby's head. While the child sleeps, sounds are made through earphones. Computers monitor brainwave activities to determine whether the baby is hearing the sounds in his or her ears.

Otoacoustic emissions (OAE): These are sounds generated from the inner ear. This test is administered by placing plugs with small microphones into a baby's ears to measure the reactions he or she has to sound.

Both processes can be completed while a baby sleeps; they take less than ten minutes to execute, and they provide no risk or potential harm to the baby being tested. If a child's hearing loss is profound, the child will be considered deaf and eligible for early intervention services that will help parents learn how to communicate with their hearing-impaired child. One of the most effective means of communication with a deaf child is sign language. Because sign language is visual, it allows the child to use his ability to learn gestural communication that will help him effectively communicate, despite an inability to hear.

> Tip:
> "A deaf or hearing-impaired child should be introduced as soon as possible to sign language if her parents wish for that to be the child's primary mode of communication."
>
> — Jill Peterson, a high school teacher from Spring, Texas

Early Detection of Hearing Loss

Often, it is not detected at birth that a child has a hearing impairment. Sometimes, it is not until a child is 2 or 3 years old that hearing loss is properly diagnosed. However, there are warning signs parents should look for in babies who may not be able to hear, including:

- Lack of attention

- Failure to verbalize sounds

- Not being startled by loud noises

- A speech delay that could be caused by hearing loss

Parents who learn their children are deaf need to take a crash course in sign language. A good place to start is by doing an Internet search of services available in your local community.

Some helpful resources for parents with deaf or hard-of-hearing children:

- **National Institute on Deafness and Other Communication Disorders** at **www.nidcd.nih.gov/health:** A national organization for deaf individuals.

- **Help Kids Hear** at **www.helpkidshear.org:** This is a site administered by a couple who has two hard-of-hearing children. The site is for parents of hard-of-hearing and deaf children, or for people who want to learn more about it.

- **American Society For Deaf Children** at **http://deafchildren.org:** A group that supports and educates families of deaf and hard-of-hearing children.

- **Parents Encouraging Parents Group:** This is a national organization of parents of children with disabilities that will be helpful with resources and information for deaf children. It has many local chapters. (For example, see **www.cde.state.co.us/cdesped/PEP. asp**.) These organizations can help put you in touch with other parents who are experiencing similar situations. Often, these groups will provide a great support system for parents and act as a resource for information about where to get services in an individual community, how to deal with particular situations, and more.

Tip:

"Only by cultural immersion can a person become fluent in sign language. And only by fluent use of the language can a person truly be a language model for children. I would suggest parents go to an interpreter training program and to sign language classes."

— Lori Dowds of Access 2 Sign Language; an interpreter who specializes in religious, performing arts, platform, and legal interpreting

Because it will be your most effective means of communicating with a hearing-impaired child, it is wise to take a full course on sign language and begin signing every day. Unlike the parent who is signing to his or her hearing baby using both spoken words and signs, the deaf child is fully relying on sign language to communicate. Though parents with hearing babies may not use sign language for every word they say, parents of deaf babies will use sign more consistently. However, because the deaf baby cannot hear sounds, it is imperative that people who sign to the baby be in his view at all times. Eye contact is essential, as the hearing baby's sight is his main way to learn about the world around him.

Did You Know?

"Deaf and hard-of-hearing children of parents who use sign, fingerspelling, and speech have higher self-esteem scores than those of deaf and hard-of-hearing children whose parents use a spoken-only method of communication."

— Dr. Petra M. Horn-Marsh, a bilingual specialist at the Kansas State School for the Deaf

Deaf Culture

Deaf culture is defined as the social movement that looks at being deaf as a difference rather than a disability. Cultural groups often stem from a group of people who have a common connection. If you relate to the deaf community but are a hearing individual, you are part of deaf culture. A person can be part of the deaf community simply if he or she sees himself or herself as part of this group of people. Often, hearing members of the deaf community are hearing parents of deaf children, deaf advocates, and people who work with and in the deaf population. Most people in this community use ASL to communicate, and sign language serves as their common link that connects them in their cultural environment.

Within the deaf community, you will find different cultures, traditions, and groups. Many members in the deaf community will associate with other members, and that is why a deaf individual may marry another deaf individual. Hence, the pair can give birth to a hearing child who has no hearing issues for all of his life but would be part of the deaf community because he was born into it.

Deaf culture is rapidly growing, but not necessarily because more babies are being born deaf. Instead, it is due to many more people's finding themselves aligned with this community of hearing-impaired individuals. In most cities across America, you will find deaf organizations that can put you in touch with the culture, especially if you are a hearing parent who raised a deaf child. The deaf community allows deaf children to be exposed early on to the culture, including the use of ASL, in all facets of their lives. From attending a deaf school to playing sports on deaf baseball or basketball teams, the culture is widespread and expanding.

Tip:

"It is important to educate hearing parents about deafness as soon as possible to prevent fear and the feeling of having to 'fix' the deaf child. Unfortunately, a majority of doctors do not have the necessary knowledge to steer parents in the direction of a more broad selection of services regarding their deaf child's future, including the use of sign language."

— Luciana Pais, a deaf interpreter based in New York City

Perhaps the biggest institutional proponent of deaf culture is Gallaudet University. This university dates back to 1856 when Amos Kendall, a postmaster general under President Andrew Jackson, set up a school for deaf and blind children in the District of Columbia. From its inception as a school that initially taught 16 children, Gallaudet University today is known for being integral in changing the face of the deaf community in the late 1980s and removing the stigma that was once associated with this culture. Currently, Gallaudet University sets the stage for the deaf community by providing "liberal education and career development for deaf and hard-of-hearing undergraduate students."

Internationally renowned, the institution of higher learning offers undergraduate and graduate programs for deaf, hard-of-hearing, and hearing students, and also conducts research into the "history, language, culture, and other topics related to deaf people." The university offers a host of graduate and undergraduate degree programs in subjects that range from accounting to economics.

Did You Know?

"Through the bilingual route, deaf and hard-of-hearing children need consistent language modeling, use, and comprehensible input in order to develop English literacy with ASL as the resource language."

— Dr. Petra M. Horn-Marsh, bilingual specialist at the Kansas State School for the Deaf

Misconceptions About Deaf Culture

Because the world largely comprises hearing societies, most hearing people hold misconceptions about the deaf culture. These misconceptions often fall under the following myths:

- **All deaf people can read lips.** Though many deaf individuals will learn how to read lips in their lifetime, many cannot solely rely on this form of communication to converse with the public. To understand how a deaf person reads lips, turn off the volume of your television and look at people moving their lips. Test yourself to see if you can catch every word that is spoken. Words that sound the same can likely be mistaken for each other. For this reason, deaf people will often use ASL as their first, native language, and read lips to reinforce this communication, or to understand those who do not know sign language and are trying to communicate with them.

- **Hearing aids allow deaf people to hear what you are saying.** Deaf people sometimes use hearing aids to magnify sound. They do not, however, allow deaf and hard-of-hearing people to hear. Hearing aids simply allow people to turn up the volume on the sounds they can already hear, which in many cases are sounds of the surrounding environment, such as a fire engine racing by or an airplane flying directly overhead.

- **Deaf people wish they could hear.** People in the deaf community have a culture all their own. Often, whole families are deaf, and they do not spend their lives in a silent world with a lack of communication. Instead, deaf people converse through sign language, body language, and in many cases, through spoken words. Most in the deaf community want to be recognized for their differences but do not want to be ostracized for being non-hearing. Those who were born deaf have been brought up in a deaf world and culture. Discrimination against a deaf person is the same as any discrimination that exists against any cultural group.

- **Deaf people can talk.** If someone is born profoundly deaf, it is rare they will develop a vocabulary and speech pattern that sounds like a hearing individual. In fact, it takes many years for deaf people to learn to speak words, including their own name. If you have never had hearing and do not know what speech sounds like, you cannot emulate it.

- **Deaf people are mentally handicapped.** Hearing and intelligence are two very different concepts. In fact, they have nothing to do with each other. Deaf people can become just as educated as hearing people, and their levels of intelligence are not measured in any way by their hearing abilities.

- **All deaf people are the same.** Just like no two people are the same, deaf people are individuals with their own beliefs, morals, and values. While they may be connected via the deaf culture, there are individual opinions, desires, and issues within the culture as there are within any other culture.

Did You Know?

"It is imperative that hearing people understand and respect sign language, and the community. If you are to benefit from knowing this beautiful language, then you also give back to the community by educating people about the community and the culture as well."

— Luciana Pais, a deaf interpreter based in New York City

If you are a hearing parent with a deaf child and you want to become a member of the deaf community, there are several easy ways to do so. Try one or all of the following:

- **Learn ASL.** This can be in a class or self-taught.

- **Seek out friendship with a deaf person.** You may find this person in your own family, at an ASL class, your church, or community.

- **Attend events to benefit the deaf community.** Learn about these events through local deaf organizations. A good place to start is with the National Association of the Deaf, **www.nad.org**, or ADARA,

Professionals Networking for Excellence in Service Delivery with Individuals who are Deaf or Hard of Hearing, **www.adara.org.**

- Volunteer your time to work with deaf children at a deaf school or local organization that works with deaf adults or children.

To fully understand deaf culture, you need to be able to confidently communicate with deaf individuals. The tools hearing people use to communicate with deaf individuals are their bodies, eye contact and, most importantly, their hands. Because deaf people cannot use words to communicate, you need to think of ways to convey the feelings you are trying to communicate. Try conveying the meaning behind these scenarios without using spoken language:

- A newborn baby's cry

- A cat scratching at a back door

- A car coming to a screeching halt

- The sound a cricket makes

- A dog's bark

- The sound of firecrackers

Parents of deaf children need to learn how to make their bodies convey emotion. Even though you want to stress intensity when signing to a hearing baby, you are still speaking words to them. In the case of a deaf child, you need to say everything in sign language. Parents with deaf children should practice showing emotion on their faces by looking in the mirror. Create expressions to convey the following feelings:

- Happiness

- Sadness

- Anger

- Fear

- Enjoyment

- Frustration

- Confusion

- Surprise

- Tiredness

- Joy/feeling overjoyed

- Shock

Did You Know?

"Children are natural language sponges; they will absorb and repeat what they see. Having someone sign to them constantly will enable them to pick it up and repeat it far more quickly than spoken words."

— Lynne Wiesman, director of Interpreter Training Program at Troy University in Troy, Alabama

Remember: If your child is deaf, ASL will be his native language. He will learn to read and write in English, and this will be his second language. Therefore, you need to be his translator for the early years. Begin communicating in ASL, and the transition to reading and writing English as your child grows will become a natural progression as well as an additional form of communication for understanding the world around him.

Controversy About Cochlear Implants

When a parent learns his or her child is deaf, it is an emotional experience. Many in the deaf community believe that to properly deal with the diagnosis, parents need to join the deaf culture. Because of this overriding feeling among those in the deaf community, there is some controversy about the usage of cochlear implants. These implants are small, intricate electronic devices that allow a person, including a child, to hear sound, even if the person is profoundly deaf. In addition to part of the implant being placed surgically under the skin, there is an external portion that rests behind the ear. The implant itself consists of a microphone, speech processor, transmitter, a receiver/stimulator, and a group of electrodes that gather and send out a signal to different parts of the auditory nerve.

Although the implant will not "cure" a person of being deaf or give him a full range of sound, it can allow a person to hear some semblance of sound in his otherwise silent world. It can also allow him to understand speech.

A cochlear implant should not be confused with a hearing aid. Hearing aids magnify sounds. Cochlear implants target the ear's auditory nerve and generate signals to the brain that help a person recognize sounds. People who wear cochlear implants do not hear the same way a person hears through his ears. In some cases, cochlear implants allow a deaf person to identify environmental sounds, such as a fast-approaching ambulance or a person on the other end of a telephone call.

Parents with children who have cochlear implants can monitor their child's hearing progress by working with an audiologist, who can run various hearing tests for the child. There also are Web sites, such as **www. VocalDevelopment.com**, that give parents examples of "baby jargon," such as cooing and babbling, so parents can begin to assess their child's language development skills. However, official tests by medical professionals should be conducted for diagnosis, as well as to monitor progress after receiving cochlear implants.

While hearing parents with deaf children may opt for cochlear implants, many people in the deaf community are truly against these implants and believe that using ASL to communicate is all a deaf child needs. The controversy also encompasses the question of whether parents have the right to decide if their child undergoes this invasive surgery — some in the deaf culture believe it should be each individual's choice. However, cochlear implants are not the only form of technology that can be used to aid a deaf or hard-of-hearing child's hearing ability. There is an array of devices that help children, especially students in a classroom, communicate better. Telecommunication devices for the deaf (TDDs) allow hearing-impaired people to use the telephone. All television sets now produced have built-in closed captioning functions. And there are many "alerting devices," which allow a deaf person to use his or her eyes to see when a doorbell or telephone is ringing, or when a baby is crying in his crib.

Hard-of-Hearing Children

Unlike being diagnosed deaf, some children are hard-of-hearing, which means they have some hearing ability. In other words, a hard-of-hearing child has hearing loss but is not completely deaf. Some hard-of-hearing children can speak, and others have limited speaking abilities.

Did You Know?

"The definition of hard-of-hearing is different for each person. For me, it means single-sided deafness. As a baby, my ear canals were unusually small, trapping infection, causing blown eardrums repeatedly to the point of deafness. The label of hard-of-hearing is as different for each person as each person's experience."

— Terri Rose, resident of Colorado Springs, Colorado, and member of the sign language interpreting field for 12 years

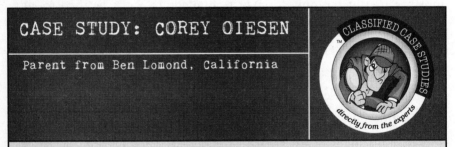

CASE STUDY: COREY OIESEN

Parent from Ben Lomond, California

Corey Oiesen is the mother of two young children. She uses sign language to help communicate with her son who, as an infant, was diagnosed with moderate sensorineural hearing loss, which is considered hard-of-hearing. She is also the president of Dovetail Public Relations and an avid genealogist. She offers her suggestions for teaching a hard-of-hearing child ASL:

1. **Start early with signs that are fun for your child.** I started with my son's favorite toy, a ball. I also taught him signs for foods, as well as "more" and "please."

2. **Speak loudly and clearly when you show your child the sign.** Make sure your child looks at your face. Hold the object for which you are signing close to your mouth when you are speaking.

3. **Enlist the help of others.** Many speech therapists and early education providers know and use sign language to help emphasize speech. Check to see if your hard-of-hearing child qualifies for

early education programs or if your medical insurance would cover sessions with a speech therapist.

4. **Once your child is familiar with the signs, practice in a noisy environment, like a restaurant.** Your child will not be able to rely on hearing you say the word. Some hard-of-hearing kids (including my son) become very reliant on the hearing that they do have and become resistant to learning signs.

5. **Stay with it.** If your child is resistant to it, do not push it, but keep using the signs. As my son grew older, he began to appreciate signed communication. He usually will not sign back to me, but he will watch for my signs. Learning sign language also helped him learn that he needs to watch a speaker's face and mouth, a very important skill for school. He needs to watch the teacher's face.

With my son, I demonstrated the sign while showing him the object I was signing, whether it be a ball or food item. I also said the word verbally in a loud, clear voice, with my hands holding the item near my mouth, so he could learn to read my lips. I also held my hands fairly close to my face when I demonstrated the sign. For abstract terms, such as "more," I used crackers to give him more when he tried the sign. "Please" became a magic word for getting the food for which he was asking.

I wish everyone in my son's life knew sign language; he would not miss anything. I am sure other parents of hard-of-hearing kids would agree that the people in a their child's life think that the child hears "just fine" or "good enough." They often do not realize that hard-of-hearing children can sometimes play along like they heard something, when they really did not. In noisy environments, such as in school, on the playground, or in sports practices, I can see that my son did not hear the instructor. He watches the other kids around him to see how they act upon the teacher's or coach's instruction. It can cause problems or misunderstandings.

I had intended to use sign language with my son before he was born, long before I knew he was hard-of-hearing. I began using signs when he was 4 or 5 months old — when he was sitting up in the high chair. His favorite toy was a ball — any type of ball. I also taught him the sign for the words "eat" and "milk." When he started to eat solid foods, I would teach the sign for each food.

I have used books, flashcards, videos, and Web sites to learn enough signs to help my son in noisy situations. Some of our signs are reprimands, such as "calm down," "sit down" and "be careful." It is tiring for me to repeat the same request over and over verbally, so I will often sign "hurry up," "please," "hurry up," and "now."

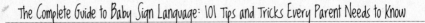
Teaching Deaf Babies ASL

From the moment your baby is born, you are caring for and introducing him to the world. You begin by showing your baby love. You hug, hold, and kiss him. These first gestures express to your baby that you love and care for him. It is important to strengthen your non-verbal bond with a baby who cannot hear.

In addition to forming an early bond with these gestures, you should cater to your child's other senses, including touch. In fact, games that require touch, such as peek-a-boo, are integral to bonding with your baby. Make sure to touch your baby, and allow him to touch you. Begin hand-over-hand signing with him to show signs when he is as young as 6 months old.

When a baby cannot hear, it is imperative that you cater to his sense of sight when you are signing. In addition to making the signs with your hands, you want to use facial expressions to convey intensity, caring, and other emotions you want to share with your baby. Use positive facial expressions, such as smiling and raised eyebrows, so babies can see your enjoyment. You want your baby to want to look at you, and soon he will be able to distinguish the emotions you are conveying through facial expressions.

Similarly, body language is important in the process of teaching your deaf or hard-of-hearing baby sign language. Be sure to use positive body language and show exaggerated emotion, such as spreading your arms wide as you prepare to hug your baby. Show him how to use gestures to convey feelings.

Parents of deaf children should interact much the same way with their baby as a parent with a hearing baby would. An onlooker at deaf parents and a deaf baby may witness exaggerated-looking movements and gestures to convey meaning. If you are a hearing parent with a deaf child, it is good to watch the interactions between a deaf parent and baby to see how you need to be profound in your gesturing and signing. You want to convey emotion without words, and catering to your baby's other senses can accomplish that.

It is important to note that using spoken words is natural for the hearing parent, and should be done especially if the baby is hard-of-hearing and can identify some sounds. You want to remain interesting to your child. In the same way a cartoon is animated, you want to be a source of enjoyment and entertainment for him. Otherwise, he may get easily distracted and lose interest in the sign language you are showing him.

To teach a deaf or hearing-impaired baby sign language, it is imperative he is in your view to see the signs you are making. It is all right to tap your child on the shoulder to get him to look in your direction — use this gentle tap in the same way you would say his name from across the room. The hearing-impaired child, if profoundly deaf, lives in a world of silence, but is often very in-tune with his other four other senses. So he will recognize the tap as your way of calling his name.

It is also important for all parents to be patient. Your child may not turn around right away or stay focused on the signs you are making. You need to go at your child's pace, not your pace. If your deaf or hard-of-hearing child is not paying attention to the signs you are making, your attempts will likely prove to be futile. For the initial months of your baby's life, he is focused on his parents, their actions, and their movements and gestures. After six months, babies will begin to focus on objects that interest them. This can be anything from a stuffed toy animal to the mobile that hangs above him in his crib.

Always follow your child's gaze to see what he is intently looking at. If you see he is staring at the family's pet cat, take this opportunity to point to the cat, and sign the word for "cat." Parents need to remain focused. At this point, you should not begin pointing to every item in the room and making the signs for them. It is likely that if you do this, your baby will start to try to follow you by moving his head in the direction of each item you are pointing to. You may confuse and overwhelm him, making sign language something that seems difficult and cumbersome. Slow down. If you learn of your child's hearing disability at a young age, you can prepare yourself and take the time needed to properly teach him this visual language.

When signing to a deaf baby as compared to a hearing baby, you may want to use ASL syntax and grammar structure because this is your baby's first language. It will be his main means of communication with you and others in her life. This is why a sign language class is recommended for hearing parents of deaf children. They are often given at local colleges, through continuing education programs at local high schools, and at some public libraries.

Like hearing babies who learn sign language, deaf babies may not sign back right away. Just like a hearing baby, it can take a deaf child six months to a year before he signs back. The difference, however, comes later, at 2 and 3 years old, when hearing babies will be speaking and deaf children most likely will not.

Tip:

"Parents of deaf children need to learn sign language themselves. Teaching isolated words is often not as effective, but learning to interact with deaf people who can teach some sentence and grammatical structures is the best way."

— Lynne Wiesman, director of Interpreter Training Program at Troy University in Troy, Alabama

CASE STUDY: SUZANNE KAMATA

Signing Parent
Japan
suekamata@msn.com

Ten years ago, Suzanne Kamata gave birth to twins. Six months later, she learned her daughter was deaf and her son was hearing. Immediately, she to learned sign language. She began learning from teachers at a deaf school her daughter now attends, from videos, and through a sign language class.

Lilia and her brother, Jio, were born 14 weeks premature. Lilia's brain was injured, and I realized that due to her cerebral palsy, we would not be going to ballet lessons. When I learned at six months that my daughter was deaf, I thought, "We will not be able to engage in girl talk." I started to mourn.

From the time that I sat next to my babies when they were born, I imagined singing and speaking to them, and that we would bond through language. I would share all of my childhood favorite books with them, and I would write stories for them in English. They would grow up bilingual, speaking my language as fluently as their father's Japanese. Though their Dad still does not understand everything I say (and vice versa) even after 12 years of marriage, I would be able to speak my native tongue at normal speed and be perfectly understood. I saw my language as a gift I could give my children.

I had never had any real contact with deaf people before my daughter's diagnosis, so I was sad, shocked, and bewildered. I cried a lot, then I started reading up on deafness. The idea of learning a new language at the age of 33 was daunting, but I quickly came to believe that it was very important for my daughter to have a language of her own, in which she could communicate with ease. Lip-reading is inexact. Some deaf adults who were raised without sign language had only a vague understanding of what was going on around them. As adults, they discovered sign language, and the world opened up.

I used sign language with both kids, and my son could use and understand signs from about 6 months old. It was also easier to understand him when he started speaking. Toddlers are not always articulate, but with the supplemental signs, we could make out what he was trying to say. It cut down on a lot of frustration.

My daughter attends a school for the deaf where all classes are conducted via sign language. As soon as I received a diagnosis, we were sent to the local deaf school. We enrolled in the early intervention program. At first, we attended once a week for about four hours, then twice a week. At the age of 3, my daughter began kindergarten.

Parents of deaf children should try to find other parents of deaf children, whether in person or online. Having peer support helps a lot. Also, try to get to know some deaf adults and learn sign language.

I used the following five tips for teaching my daughter sign language:

1. Make up a sign for your child's name and other family members' names.

2. Make sure you have your child's attention before you try to communicate.

3. Remember that facial expressions are part of sign language; it is not just the hands.

4. Remember that deaf children do not pick up words the way that hearing children do. Try to input as much vocabulary as possible. Narrate your actions. For example, sign, "Now I am going to pick up the fork that you dropped."

5. If you do not know the sign for something, make up a "home sign" to use temporarily. For cheese, I used to sign "mouse" and then "food."

Because they cannot hear, deaf children gather most information visually. In a learning environment, it is more difficult for deaf children to concentrate. Research has shown that deaf children who grow up with deaf parents who sign are at an advantage over those who grow up in hearing, non-signing families. If possible, other family members should learn to sign, too. At my daughter's school, the teachers use sign language when speaking to hearing mothers for this same reason.

Like Kamata, many parents of deaf children need access to resources that will help them communicate with their children. Parents need to keep in mind that teaching sign language to a deaf baby is similar to the way in which you would teach it to a hearing baby. When the child is interested in the ASL signs shown to him, he is more likely to use ASL. It is also wise to introduce new signs relative to a particular topic to continue to introduce signs. For example, if you are making dinner in the kitchen and your baby is watching you from a playpen or bouncy seat, show him the signs for "kitchen," "sink," "refrigerator," "pan," and "stove."

Through her research, Dr. Patricia Elizabeth Spencer, who wrote a book on conversing with deaf and hard-of-hearing children, measured responsiveness in the language of hearing mothers with deaf babies, hearing mothers with hearing babies, and deaf mothers with deaf babies. Her results found that mothers, in general, "followed their baby's interest about 80 percent of the time."

This is a good measure of what hearing parents of deaf children should do. Although you may not have the option of being responsive 100 percent of the time to what your baby is focused on, you need to be in tune with your baby at least 80 percent of the time. What this means is that when you see what it is that your baby is interested in, stay with that focus. It is best to teach sign language within these focused moments because this is when your baby senses your responsiveness to her interests, and she will be more eager to learn new signs.

Body Movement

In her research, Spencer also wrote that it is important for parents to notice arm and leg movements. Parents need to recognize when their baby is excited and interested. If he flails his arms when his grandmother walks into the room, it is likely this means he is happy to see this person. This is also the time to sign the word "Grandma." Whenever your child uses her body parts to convey emotion, cater to that. If she kicks her legs when she wants to be picked up, show you understand her by picking her up. Deaf children need to be understood by their parents; the sooner the bonding and understanding begins, the better the communication will be, and the more likely the baby will learn sign language with ease.

However, constant ASL teaching can become cumbersome. Babies, like all adults, need downtime — so take a break from teaching sign. Show love to your baby with gestures, such as hugging. There is no rush in teaching your child ASL, as most hearing babies will not speak before 10 months to 2 years of age. Therefore, if your child was diagnosed deaf, give him time to be exposed to and learn sign language. If babies are over-stimulated, they may tend to pay less attention to your actions, thus not focusing on the signs you are making.

Methods for Teaching ASL to Deaf and Hard-of-Hearing Children

The following are a few basic exercises to teach sign language to your child who is deaf or hard-of-hearing:

- A great way to teach hearing-impaired children sign language is to use pictures. By showing your child a picture, and then making the sign, you are explaining to him its meaning as you would explain to a hearing baby with spoken words. Stick to one topic and stay focused on this topic. Teach signs and show him how the pictures relate. If you show him the sign for "cat" by pointing at your household pet, take out a book of signs relating to animals. Maybe start with those that have something in common, such as fur; show him photos of dogs, cats, and bears. Then illustrate the signs for those words.

- Point or tap on an object several times when making the sign for it. This will allow your baby to learn the sign and recognize the object for the sign. It will allow him to learn what communication is all about.

- Hold objects close to your face when you are "talking" via ASL about the objects. This is most beneficial for the deaf or hard-of-hearing baby because you cannot use spoken words to communicate with your child. He needs to see you and the object you are talking about through sign language. You need to make eye contact with him, and he needs to see your facial expressions and other body language.

- Develop signals through touch that will allow your baby to know you want to talk to him. Whether it is gently tapping the shoulder or gently caressing his arm with your fingertips, come up with a touch-based signal that will allow your child to realize you need to communicate with him. Use this signal consistently so it is effective. Other members of the family should adapt to using this signal. Eventually, your baby will know who is tapping. Parents need to know babies will not recognize this signal early on. It takes time, just like it takes time for a hearing child to properly pronounce words.

- Use repetition frequently. Be sure to show your child the signs for objects in his world over and over. This reinforces the meaning of the signs. Every time you give your baby a bottle, sign "bottle," and "milk." Just like a hearing baby will use these signs when he wants a bottle or milk, a baby who cannot hear will do the same. However, he needs to also understand the meaning for the signs, and the only way to do this is by repetition.

- Initiate short phrases in ASL. Just as a hearing family would begin to teach their child a short phrase once the child could talk, the deaf child will need to be introduced to phrases as he begins to learn sign language. These short phrases can be introduced as early as birth but should be focused on after the baby has begun to sign. For example, your son may begin to use signs for his basic needs and wants by the age of 8 months. Once he is using several signs regularly, it is time to teach him to sign short phrases. So instead of only signing "more" when he wants more crackers, teach him the signs for "more crackers please."

Once a deaf child has learned to sign, it is important to continue to introduce sign language to your child because this is his only form of communication. At this point, you may want to teach her how to ask questions the way your hearing 2-year-old may ask, "Where is Daddy or Mommy?" You need to allow your deaf child to be inquisitive about the things in life that he wants to know more about. For this reason, teach your child how to ask questions early on in sign language.

In addition to modeling sign language and teaching ASL at home, you should send a deaf child to sign language instruction with professionals. Some type of formal education setting often helps jumpstart early communication skills, such as one-on-one teaching or in a class for hearing-impaired children.

In many cases, deaf children are put in mainstream classrooms, and they utilize the services of a deaf interpreter to learn along with hearing peers. Very often, the interpreter will stand in front of the classroom and translate English language into ASL for a deaf child.

Children of Deaf Adults

A hearing child can be born to two deaf parents, or one deaf and one hearing parent. So how can a hearing child with deaf parents learn English and sign language? The deaf child will likely have his first language as ASL. For this reason, the English spoken language becomes his second language, and he will likely be bilingual from a very young age. If he has two deaf parents, they will begin signing every word to him at birth. He will learn this visual language in the same way a deaf child would learn it. However, it is likely the hearing baby of deaf parents will have many family members who will speak to them verbally. This is where the baby will begin to learn verbal language. The deaf parents will also be conscious of exposing the child to verbal language by letting the child watch television and listen to the radio.

If a deaf child is born to deaf parents, sign language will be the natural language used in the home. And, in many cases, it is taught much like how hearing parents with hearing babies would teach spoken words.

Did You Know?

"Hearing children of deaf adults (also known as CODAs) enjoy linguistic and cognitive advantages of being bilinguals. Their language development is rich in vocabulary, syntax, and concept flexibility, and bilinguals have deeper metalinguistic knowledge and understanding of their first and second languages."

— Dr. Petra M. Horn-Marsh, bilingual specialist at the Kansas State School for the Deaf

CASE STUDY: PETRA M. HORN-MARSH, PH.D

Kansas State School for the Deaf
450 E. Park St.
Olathe, Kansas 66061
Phone number: 913-791-0505
E-mail: phorn@ksd.state.ks.us

CLASSIFIED CASE STUDIES™
directly from the experts

Dr. Petra M. Horn-Marsh is a bilingual specialist (certified teacher for the D/HH, bachelor's degree in secondary education and history, master's degree in history, and a Ph.D. in sociology). Signing since birth, she was born to deaf parents who moved to the United States from Germany. After she completed her undergraduate studies at Gallaudet University, she began work as a research assistant in the Bellugi Lab at Salk Institute to develop research experiments in ASL to be used with deaf, hard-of-hearing, and hearing subjects who are native and non-native ASL users.

I began my employment at Kansas State School as the bilingual specialist at for the deaf, after completing my doctorate studies and a three-year stint as a school administrator. I conducted ASL assessments with all kindergarten through 12th-grade students, developing ASL goals for deaf and hard-of-hearing students who demonstrate language delays, disorders, or needs. I also taught an ASL immersion class with kindergarten students who have delays in ASL. I am also a mother of five children (three of them are hearing and two of them are deaf), and they all are native ASL users.

Acquiring ASL as a language (rather than learning signs on a word level) and then acquiring English allows the child to enjoy the cognitive and linguistic benefits of bilingualism as long as the child uses both languages. However, when the child ceases to use ASL, the child already has the cognitive flexibility to learn another language with fluency. Fluency happens when a person uses the language on a regular basis. There are various levels of bilingualism, trilingualism, and multilingualism based on the frequency of and fluency in language use.

My special niche and specialty is language delay and language disorders in deaf and hard-of-hearing children. This also can apply to hearing children who have speech disorders and may benefit from ASL. Regardless, the majority of deaf and hard-of-hearing children are not allowed to acquire or become proficient in ASL; consequently, many of them arrive in school severely delayed in language and communication abilities. When untreated (without ASL tutoring, immersion, and/or language support services), these children's language delays then become language disorders either in primary or secondary, depending on years of language neglect and communication abuse. This could occur from a lack of resolution to these issues in a child's younger years when it could have been more easily corrected. These unfortunate phenomena have an impact on their cognition. Language and cognition are interdependent. It is my desire to collect a large database supporting the argument in ensuring that deaf and hard-of-hearing infants and children have regular and consistent access to ASL. It is also my desire to use the data to inform the public, parents, and educators on the importance of legislating deaf and hard-of-hearing infants and children's rights to ASL. This will ensure that their right to a complete and natural language will not be taken away from them.

Children develop the ability to communicate fluently, play with language, become creative with language, and express themselves using various genres and registers. Through fluent communication, they also enjoy watching me "story sign" (read aloud) and learning how to read in addition to learning and discussing various social and academic topics.

Chapter Eleven

Becoming a
Sign Language Professional

I f baby sign language has you thinking about what you can do with all the ASL skills you just taught yourself, you may consider pursuing a career in sign language. This chapter will explore careers you can pursue in your sign language journey. If this has become more of a passion than a pastime for you, there are many ways to further your education of ASL and use it to help others.

Careers in ASL

There are several careers that you can pursue if you are fluent in ASL. Following is a general listing:

- **Interpreter:** There are many opportunities for translating English into ASL for deaf people. Many colleges offer both associate's and bachelor's degrees in interpreting. To become an educational interpreter, you will have to take and pass the Educational Interpreter Performance Assessment to become certified in this field. The EIPA is a national standard video assessment of an interpreter's skills.

Classroom Interpreting's Web site provides an overview of what you will need to learn about the test at **www.classroominterpreting.org**. You will be assessed in four major areas:

- o Intonational, grammatical, and spatial representation (used when signing)

- o Ability to read child/teen sign language

- o Sign vocabulary

- o Pragmatic representation/overall behaviors

- **Teacher or administrator of deaf programs or schools:** There are many programs that specifically teach deaf children ASL. These programs can be found in public schools, private schools, and in daycare and preschool populations. Many people who pursue degrees in special education will obtain additional credentials to be able to teach deaf children. Often, these teachers will be required to have a master's degree in special education. An administrator of a special school for deaf children would be more involved in the operation and function of the school. This would require a strong bond with the deaf community and working with deaf parents and students. For this reason, such an administrator will have to be fluent in ASL and know about the needs of those in the deaf community.

- **Tutor:** Just like children who are hearing, many deaf students need tutoring assistance in a variety of subjects. Though tutors in deaf schools or programs would be required to communicate in sign language with their students, many tutors affiliated with mainstream schools also learn signing to cater to the deaf population attending the schools.

- **College professor:** Any college or university that offers ASL programs, classes, or degrees for interpreters utilize college professors who have a background in ASL. In addition, college professors proficient in ASL are needed to teach deaf classes. There are several universities around the country that cater to a deaf population, such as Gallaudet University in Washington, D.C.

- **Adjunct professor:** In many cases, those people who have had a successful career as an interpreter will become an adjunct professor at a college that offers ASL courses. There are professors who are not on staff but teach a few classes a semester and are highly regarded due to their experience in a particular industry.

- **Dorm attendant:** Boarding schools or colleges that cater to a deaf population need people proficient in ASL to communicate with students living in a dormitory atmosphere.

- **Actor:** Sign language abilities can also be put to good use in an entertainment forum. There are theater and dance performance groups that perform in sign language. If you are a budding actor and have sign language skills, you may be able to combine your two passions.

- **Private or public sector interpreter:** You may be asked to work for a public official or a private company to translate to deaf participants at a meeting or public event. You could be hired to sign the national anthem or Pledge of Allegiance at specific events.

Sign Language Interpreting

One of the most recognized careers in the sign language field is an interpreter. Today, many colleges and universities across the country offer bachelor's degrees in this field. These allow you to become fluent in ASL and to become a translator between deaf and English-speaking people. Interpreters are used in various settings, from government agencies and classrooms to nursing homes and hospitals. Anywhere a deaf person needs a translator, an interpreter can be used. Interpreters can be hired by government agencies and be on hand to translate at events such as an official's speech at local town hall meetings. Many times, people such as students at a college will hire deaf interpreters. This interpreter would attend all the students' classes with him and translate every word the English-speaking professor says into ASL for the student.

A sign language interpreter also has various avenues to pursue for work. Often, the following opportunities are available once a degree has been obtained in sign language interpreting:

Ways to work as an interpreter

- **Freelance:** This is when you set yourself up in your own sign language interpreting business, and take clients as your schedule allows. You are your own boss and work as little, or as much, as you desire. However, it may be tough to attract clients if you begin your career in this fashion. Very often, freelance interpreters go out on their own to start a freelance career after working for an agency in some capacity and after obtaining several years of experience in the industry. After a few years in this business, you likely will have developed good networking skills, which will help attract clients.

- **A referral agency:** You are your own individual contractor but work for an agency, which will offer you a referral. So someone who is in need of a deaf interpreter will call a referral agency, which recommends you for services. You are not employed by the referral agency but essentially receive work from them. This is not much different from freelancing, but you devote your time to taking clients from a specific agency. The business or person who is hiring the interpreter pays the agency, and the agency, in turn, pays the interpreter.

- **Interpreting agency:** In this case, a company that will provide you with work in different areas will employ you. You may choose to specialize in a particular setting, such as classroom instruction, and will work with specific clients of the agency. Agencies will help promote your services and allow you to have the most exposure of your services.

Did You Know?

"Agencies determine how much interpreters get paid versus how much they charge the business. Overhead costs may include insurance, office equipment and space, office personnel, Web site maintenance, continuing education, and such. I believe most agencies will figure an approximate 15 to 30 percent off the top of what they charge businesses for their own costs and profit margins. The bulk of what agencies charge goes out to interpreters' pay."

— Lori Dowds, personnel director, Access 2 Sign Language

Each state has different licensing requirements for interpreters. Often, you can apply for certification upon receiving a college degree in interpreting. According to the U.S. Department of Labor, approximately 22 percent of interpreters and translators are self-employed, many of whom work part-time. Most interpreters possess a bachelor's degree and fluency in at least two languages.

> **Tip:**
>
> "Check your state to see how interpreters are credentialed or licensed. Also check other professional outlets like Registry of Interpreters for the Deaf (**www.RID.org**) or American Sign Language Teachers Association (**www. ASLTA.org**). If your school district or doctor's office is providing teachers/interpreters for you, ask about their credentials."
>
> — Terri Rose of Access 2 Sign Language

Sign language interpreters have a special alignment to the deaf community. Most were not born deaf, and they work in the community for profit. For this reason, they are often considered deaf culture "special members," who foster the advancements of the community.

> **Did You Know?**
>
> "Another setting for interpreters to work is for one of the national Video Relay Service (VRS) companies, interpreting for deaf people on video phones for them to make phone calls to hearing people. Most VRS companies require RID certification, which is prohibitive for most new interpreters to obtain. VRS does hire full-time employees with benefits; however, positions are limited."
>
> — Lori Dowds, personnel director of Access 2 Sign Language

CASE STUDY: LUCIANA PAIS

Freelance Interpreter
84-12 Cuthbert Rd #2
Kew Gardens, New York 11415
(949) 306-1883
lullapais@aol.com
RID CI (Certification of Interpretation for Registry of Interpreters for the Deaf)

A freelance interpreter in New York City for the past five years, Luciana Pais was born to deaf parents in Brazil and learned Brazilian sign language (known as "Libras") at the same time she learned spoken Portuguese. After moving to the United States 20 years ago, she also learned ASL and after a few years decided to pursue a career in interpreting, She joined the LaGuardia Community College Interpreting Program and after graduating began freelancing, She also provides some support to the interpreting/deaf community in Brazil.

Both my parents were the only deaf members of their families, and the only ones who used sign language. Growing up, I saw firsthand how important the job of a language interpreter is and how fortunate I was to have had the exposure to deaf culture from the perspective of an "insider."

For my job, I provide accurate interpretation between users of sign language and non-signers. Part of the process includes message equivalency, cultural equivalency, and linguistic equivalency as well.

There are many opportunities to work in the ASL interpreter field in both the public and private sector. Legislation in the United States has provided important opportunities to the deaf regarding access to education and information through various means. Interpreting is an important part of granting access to deaf individuals, and the most recent piece of legislation that has had a strong impact in the lives of deaf people is the American with Disabilities Act (ADA) of 1990. Among many provisions, it requires "employers to provide reasonable accommodations to the known disability of a qualified applicant or employee." That has sparked a demand for interpreters, as well as interpreting programs, in order to comply with the law.

There are many different areas in interpreting. I myself have found a niche in medical interpreting. I mostly work at hospitals, and my assignments include surgeries, consultations, cancer treatments, rehabilitation, labor and delivery, diabetes clinics, and everything else that comes up in a medical setting. But one can find many different niches, such as musical shows, college classes, the public school system, legal settings, and more.

The most rewarding part of my job is to see communication happen. I enjoy seeing a message accurately delivered. My greatest moment working with a person relating to sign language was not actually at work, but instead happened in one of those magical New York moments. I was walking on a beautiful fall evening when I noticed a gorgeous full moon, over a path of the trains, and the lights were fantastic. The next person I made eye contact with passed by me, and I could not help but to mention how beautiful the moon was. In a split second, the same person said the word "deaf," advising me she had not heard what I said. I was pleased to put my books down and sign to this person exactly what I wanted to share: that the moon was gorgeous that night, and she agreed. It was about ten seconds, but at that moment, I realized how awesome it was that I knew sign language and that I could communicate with a deaf person.

One of the biggest challenges I face on the job is the lack of knowledge about the existence of a deaf culture and a deaf community. Most of the hearing world do not see deaf people as part of a linguistic minority that use sign language. It is a process of educating people to treat deaf culture as a culture, with its own language, customs, and proper characteristics.

With that, we often become educators of the culture and the language. This is a delicate balance because we interpreters are also hearing. We are part of that majority that has oppressed the deaf, but we are also allies in the cause. When I interpret in medical settings, I deal with doctors, nurses, and deaf consumers. Much of the time, the doctor or nurse will speak to me and not to the deaf patient. I must, in a subtle way, make clear that they should be speaking directly to patient. That is one of the most common situations I encounter in my interpreting jobs — the lack of knowledge of deaf culture.

The success stories are the ones in which the consumers have gotten the message: the doctor who was able to understand the symptoms, the child who was able to understand the joke of the clown in the circus, the drug addict who was able to express his desire to detox. All of these are success stories because if there were no interpreters, the outcome could have been a lot different.

Sign Language Interpreter: The Intermediary

Because a sign language interpreter is the intermediary between a deaf person and a person who is trying to communicate with him or her, the interpreter plays an integral role. This job is one that allows a deaf person the freedom to communicate with members of the public who do not know ASL. However, pursuing a career in sign language interpreting is not as easy as one may think. It is a job where you may find yourself on your feet all day, standing in front of a classroom, an audience, or in an assembly hall, translating every word that is spoken by a teacher, judge, elected official, or actress. To be successful in the job, you must possess keen listening skills, the ability to grasp concepts with ease, the ability to focus, the ability to explain, and the ability to think clearly.

An interpreter for the deaf is not only translating spoken words into sign language, but it is also their job to relate concepts and meaning behind those words. So if a teacher is teaching a math lesson and the interpreter is translating for a deaf individual, it is important that the interpreter relays the teacher's concepts and explanations of the math problems.

Because of this, when possible, it is imperative that interpreters do their homework and read up or at least familiarize themselves with the subjects they will be translating prior to a day of work.

There are two basic methods for interpreting:

- **Simultaneous interpretation:** This method is when interpreters listen and sign at the same time. The translation occurs simultaneously, so the deaf person is learning through sign language what his or her peers hear through spoken words at the very same time. It is not uncommon for interpreters to simultaneously work in pairs, switching off every half-hour for a break. These types of interpreters are often used at large speaking engagements, national events, in government or court settings, and televised conferences.

- **Consecutive interpretation:** This process occurs when the sign language interpreter begins to sign after a person has spoken several words or a whole sentence. Some interpreters who use two consecutive methods take shorthand notes while listening to a speaker talk. This type of interpreting often occurs in more intimate settings, very often in one-on-one situations.

Did You Know?

"A big challenge comes when hearing people do not understand interpreters are professionals. We are not personal friends of our deaf customers, are not their 'helpers,' and [are] in no way responsible for them. Often, in ignorance, people think we are somehow the deaf person's disability caretaker, or that we are volunteers helping these 'poor unfortunates.'"

— Lori Dowds, personnel director of Access 2 Sign Language

CASE STUDY: LORI DOWDS

Personnel Director
Access 2 Sign Language
PO Box 15433
Colorado Springs, Colorado 80935
(719) 302-5869
2ServeU@MyA2SL.com

Lori Dowds became involved with sign language when her oldest son, now 19 years old, was found to be severely speech delayed at the age of 3. She later learned he had Asperger syndrome. A few years later, she went back to school to become a sign language interpreter. She earned an interpreting degree at Pikes Peak Community College in May 2000 and also has a bachelor's degree in sociology from the University

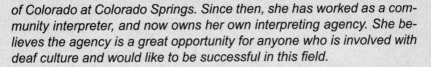

of Colorado at Colorado Springs. Since then, she has worked as a community interpreter, and now owns her own interpreting agency. She believes the agency is a great opportunity for anyone who is involved with deaf culture and would like to be successful in this field.

I learned signs to help my son communicate, and I became an interpreter just because I think it is fun. I did not have an altruistic motivation — it was for sheer joy that I took up this work and continue to do so. In June 2005, I married my second husband, Michael, a deaf man who was raised in the oral method and learned sign language as an adult.

The oral method is used when deaf children are taught to lip read and speak. My husband was given extensive speech training as a child. The philosophy often includes a belief that if a deaf child is also taught to sign while receiving speech training, he will not learn to speak and will take the easy way out signing.

My husband was exposed to minimal signs using Signing Exact English, which is an artificially created sign system used to teach deaf children English, and did not learn ASL until college when he chose to attend the National Technical Institute for the Deaf. Michael now inspires me to stretch my skills and professionalism, but I still do the work just for fun.

Because I am now an owner of an interpreter agency, I schedule interpreters, interview with interpreters signing up to work with us, and contract with interpreters. I think a lot of my job is to set the standards of what we consider professional, ethical behavior and how we treat our customers and each other with respect. I work in the field as an interpreter and work in teams with many of our contractors. It bridges the gap between those working in the community and our office.

As an interpreter, I specialize (if you can truly be specialized in multiple areas) in religious, performing arts, platform, and legal interpreting. I work hard to keep up with the latest in our field, including the best practices and what laws have changed in our state that impacts interpreters. I attend numerous workshops and meetings of various organizations, such as the Colorado Commission for the Deaf and Hard of Hearing. I strive to continually improve my own skills and credentials, including my recent legal qualification. I am involved in the Colorado RID mentoring program.

Employment opportunities for interpreters include educational, community/agency, and video relay service interpreting (VRS). Interpreters can work directly for schools, from kindergarten to grade 12, and colleges and universities. They tend to pay less than any other setting, but it is a great for an interpreter starting out; you may get benefits as well. Many states now require kindergarten to grade 12 educational interpreters to obtain an Educational Interpreter Performance Assess-ment (EIPA) credential.

To work in the community, many locations require you to have RID certification, which is difficult for new interpreters to obtain. Also, most jobs working for agencies are for independent contractors, so there are no guaranteed hours or benefits. There are the rare positions available to work for one company that may have several deaf people in need of interpreting, but often those positions include job descrip-tions where you would be an interpreter/office assistant or have some such additional duties.

Many interpreters use a combination of two or more of the above op-tions. I work through my agency as well as supplement my income by working, on average, one day a week for Purple Communications as a VRS interpreter.

I love to interpret for plays. I feel as though deaf people get to experience culture in a visual form when they go to plays. My favorite play was "The Gruffalo," performed by a British troupe for school children from across the city. It was the first time the troupe had a sign language interpreter for a performance, and they were very excited and supportive. They took me backstage and showed me what the Gruffalo costume looked like so I could portray it accurately. Then they sang some of the songs so I could get more of a feel for the music instead of just the words I had read on the script. Finally, the troupe helped me come up with a sign for the Gruffalo. They were so proud to be a part of the effort to bring this play to deaf children. When it came time to perform, their collabora-tion with me created something magical. The deaf children were able to "feel" the play so much more than they would have with just the words. I could see the children's reactions and participation in the story. I was very proud of our work that day.

My favorite experience working directly with a deaf child was when I was substitute teaching in a preschool for two weeks. A child had multiple disabilities, and I was very concerned I would not be able to communi-cate with her. It turned out to be a very precious experience. The child was able to understand me quite well. I struggled to understand her, but her classmates all signed some and were very helpful teaching me their classroom signs. She got along well with the other children and was treated no differently from the others. She treated me much like the teacher or aide in the class, at times wanting my attention and assis-tance, other times ready to push me away and be with her friends. It was thrilling to me to see how well she was integrated into this classroom with the other children.

More Careers That Use Sign Language

Although a career in sign language interpreting can be both rewarding and profitable, there are many other ways you can utilize ASL skills in a professional work environment. For example, many schools for the deaf utilize sign language professionals for many different positions, such as teacher aides, secretaries, and school campus administrators. Though a deaf school administer will often have a education-related degree, there are many courses that universities and colleges across the country offer to budding sign language professionals. Often, someone pursuing a teacher's degree will take sign language interpreting classes that will qualify him or her to work with deaf students in programs and in deaf schools. In some cases, a person who already holds a bachelor's degree in education may want to then pursue an interpreter's degree. Each state, and each organization or entity, has different regulations for the educational background a person needs to obtain a position where sign language will be the main form of communication with students. It is wise to explore different colleges and the options each offers to students. Also, ask what jobs alumni have obtained from the degree program, so you can learn about the opportunities that exist for the particular type of training you will receive.

CASE STUDY: LYNNE WIESMAN

Owner of Signs of Development
Director, Interpreter Training Program
College of Education, Troy Campus
317 Hawkins Hall, Troy University
334-670-3361 | 334-670-3548 (fax)
LWiesman@troy.edu
http://troy.troy.edu/education/itpin-
dex.html

Lynne Wiesman has devoted her life to sign language. She believes a career in the sign language community is one that can be filled with accomplishment and success. She also says there continues to be a great need for sign language interpreters. Currently, she is a master mentor and holds certifications from the National Registry of Interpreters for the Deaf (CI/CT and SC:L) and Court Interpreter Certification from the Board for Certification of Interpreters in Texas. Academically, Lynne received her associate's degree from Southwest Collegiate Institute for the Deaf in Big Spring, Texas; bachelor's degree in organizational leadership; and master's in business administration from Maryville University. She is A.B.D. (All But Dissertation), working toward her Ph.D. in training and performance improvement, and has research interests in mentoring to close the graduation-to-certification performance gap.

I have been signing for more than 25 years. My grandfather was deaf and did not sign, but I grew up making things visual for him. I attended a small college in West Texas for deaf people (although I am not deaf) called SouthWest Collegiate Institute for the Deaf. Being only one of a few who could hear, refusing an interpreter, and already having a more heightened sensitivity to communicating visually, I acquired ASL in a few months, sufficient to take and pass the Texas interpreting certification exam. Since 1985, I have interpreted and directed numerous programs related to sign language and interpreting.

At Troy University, we have a four-year program to become a deaf interpreter that can be taken completely online or on campus. It is the only interpreter training program in the state, and one of the only programs in the nation offering a Bachelor of Arts and Bachelor of Science degree, as well as the only program that has a full Interpreter Training Program (ITP) onsite and online. Graduates will earn a Bachelor of Science and can become sign language interpreters in a variety of settings, including but not limited to:

Video relay services (VRS)

Department of Mental Health

Department of Education

Local interpreting agency, either as a freelance/independent contractor, or as a part-time or full-time member

Social services

ADRS services

This industry still has a very high demand and low supply, so it has not been adversely impacted by the recession. It is a great career for someone to pursue at this time, when many other industries are not hiring people, and instead making budget cuts.

Become a BSL Expert

Throughout this book, you have read testimonies from parents who used ASL to communicate with their preverbal or deaf babies and then took the knowledge to teach sign language. After receiving a sign language accreditation, you will be certified to teach baby sign language classes. There are many private, for-profit companies that offer classes, including, but not restricted to:

- Sign2Me, **www.sign2me.com/index.php**

- Kindersigns, **www.kindersigns.com/bizopps.htm**

- Baby Signs, **www.babysigns.com**

Each of these companies can prepare you to teach basic baby sign language classes to mothers and children. If you would prefer to teach children directly or in a daycare setting, you may have additional requirements, such as a college degree. If you choose to open your own "Daddy/Mommy & Me" class or children's program in sign language, you will need a recreational, fun space to conduct classes. Usage of props is key to keep babies and children interested.

If you have never been in a teaching situation before, it is wise to attend some baby sign language classes first to see how classes are conducted, and learn the key ways to teach sign language to children and their parents. Though there are no college degrees in baby sign language, it would be wise to be fluent in ASL, even if you plan to only teach basic baby sign language classes. If a mother or father asks to learn a particular sign, you will want to know how to illustrate it. For this reason, it is wise to have a broad sign language vocabulary before teaching sign language classes.

Tip:

"Sign language is not a highly regulated field, so it is up to you to determine what is best for your child and your long-term goals. Then work with professionals who can assist you in attaining those goals."

— Terri Rose of Access 2 Sign Language

CASE STUDY: JUDI ROCKHILL

Owner, Signing Family
Silver Spring
judirockhill@gmail.comm

Judi Rockhill is the owner and an instructor for Signing Family, Capital Sign Language Services, which is a sign language interpreting agency. She launched Signing Family in 2004 after having great success teaching her own twins' sign language. Most of her classes are held in people's homes. Sometimes they are small classes, just for one family; sometimes they are large classes, such as a neighborhood playgroup or a church group. She is also a sign language interpreter who has interpreted for presidents of large companies, doctors, lawyers, hospice patients, concerts, and more.

I could fingerspell as a child and had a signing vocabulary of about 25 signs. I did not really learn the language until I graduated from high school and met a deaf friend who taught me sign. I continued taking local sign language classes at churches and evening school programs until I found the Community College of Philadelphia and enrolled in their interpreter education program.

I earn my living signing. I have been interpreting for about 18 years and teaching for about five years. My twins used twin-speak instead of English. I could not understand them unless they said a word I taught them, such as "Mommy" or "Daddy." We decided to teach them signing to bridge their language with ours. The results were amazing. Fast-forward about five years, and they started school in a French immersion program with no French language experience at all. We fully believe their ability to sign helped them with their French acquisition. They were certainly more open to using another language because of it.

Sign language is such a part of my life; in addition to the linguistic benefits, I wanted my children to understand that deaf kids (or hearing kids who have deaf parents) need to be understood, too. I wanted to develop in them an understanding of the world around them, and that includes disabilities.

The most important thing I have learned from teaching sign language is to set up realistic expectations for parents. During my first class, I had a family who was very

disappointed that their 4- or 5-month-old triplets would not be able to tell them when they had an earache. I realized the parents had unrealistic expectations and have since clarified them before each class. Parents have never told me anything negative about teaching their kids to sign. I have heard great success stories and less-successful stories, but no complaints.

I had one student, about 5 years old, who had speech issues and could not communicate well with her family. I was hired to do a series of classes with them. Between my class and the child's school resources, the family began to understand her needs.

My classes are offered to everyone. I make my classes affordable and short-term so there is not a huge time or money investment. The people who continue my classes are there because they want to be — not because they paid for a 10-week class and feel as though they need to attend because of that.

Learning signing has given my own kids an understanding of language and communication in general that many other kids did not have. Once they realized that I could understand them, they never stopped signing and talking, and their frustrations were significantly reduced. Signing really helped in their transition from twin-speak to English. And later, as they were beginning in a French-immersion program, more benefits became clear: My kids' acceptance of another language was easier than their classmates. I firmly believe it helped them in their second spoken language. I have no idea if it is because, as the studies show, the synapses in the brain started working earlier, but I do know that they had smoother transition than their classmates who had learned only one language.

I have taught many families beginning sign language, and each one has been encouraged to continue signing with their kids. I am lucky enough to live in Washington, D.C., which is home to a large deaf population. By coming to my classes, the participants have learned not only how to sign, but why it is important. During my classes, we discuss the importance of using sign language interpreters and why this is a good career choice — hopefully inspiring the next generation of interpreters.

When someone who has been struggling to remember a sign or just was not understanding the sign suddenly comprehends, that is an "a-ha" moment. My greatest joy comes from the older kids — aged 3 to 5 — who get it and use it. It is great to see the light bulb come on, and a concept become clear.

Chapter Twelve

Sign Language for
Home and Public Schooling

Because of all the benefits of using sign language with babies and toddlers who are learning to read and spell, many teachers today choose to integrate sign language into classroom lessons. This chapter will provide helpful classroom exercises and suggestions for ways elementary school teachers can integrate sign language into the classroom. Home-school parents can also integrate these sign language lessons into their schooling if six or more students get together for the lessons.

Preschool teachers will often start to teach sign language in much of the same way that you teach your preverbal baby: Saying the word and making the sign simultaneously is how many teach this language. One way many preschool teachers will introduce sign language to students is during "circle time" songs, in which students may sign all the words to childhood favorite songs. Because children at this age begin to mimic the actions teachers and other adults show them, they enjoy making these gestures. Toddlers and children who have never been exposed to sign language in the home will often find it fun, new, and exciting to learn signs that they can go home to share with Mom and Dad. In addition, sign language used in kindergarten, first, second, and even higher grades can be used to help the students bond, keep them focused, and facilitate reading, spelling, and bilingualism.

Some helpful tools to integrate sign language into your classroom:

- Sign language flashcards

- A sign language alphabet chart

- Sign language instructional DVDs

However, most of the materials needed to teach sign language to your students are already in your classroom. This chapter will serve as your complete resource for how to integrate it into your early childhood classroom.

Teaching Students About Deaf Culture

Your early childhood or elementary school students who have never been part of a signing household will be unfamiliar with the language and its usage. For this reason, they need to be taught the importance of deaf culture: that sign language is another language for them to learn, and that it will help them communicate with other people who sign, including deaf people. While you may explain to your students that deaf people cannot hear, this may open a wide spectrum of questions. To help your students understand the concept of being deaf, you can use various children's books that address the topic, such as:

- *I'm Deaf and It's OK* (Lorraine Aseltine, Evelyn Mueller, and Nancy Tait, 1986): This book is about a young boy who wears a hearing aid. He becomes angry when he learns that he will always need a hearing aid, but a deaf friend at school helps him realize he can do many things despite having to wear the hearing aid.

- *Moses Goes To School* (Isaac Millman, 2000): Attending a school for deaf children, young Moses in this story learns ASL and uses it to communicate with his peers.

In addition, it may be helpful to:

- Have your students interact with deaf children.

- Visit a deaf school in your community.

- Before the trip to the school, have your children learn some signs such as, "Hi, my name is..." or simply "hello," "goodbye," and "nice to meet you."

Students being taught ASL in the classroom need to recognize these visual signs as more than a lesson taught by the teacher. The children need to recognize that this is a complete language used by many people to communicate, specifically those who identify themselves as being part of deaf culture.

In the classroom, teachers can perform exercises to allow children to understand deaf culture. An example of this would be to have the teacher mouth a lesson as if she were speaking, but without any verbal sounds. At the same time, she should use sign language to communicate with students. This brings the children into a world without sound and helps them understand how sign language is used in the deaf community.

If it is possible to have deaf students join a classroom lesson, the teacher can communicate via ASL with the deaf students and have them communicate to the teacher and among each other using sign language. Again, this will submerge hearing students in a "deaf world" and help them better understand how ASL is truly a language that helps people who cannot communicate like they do.

The interaction with deaf students will allow your hearing students to fully understand the use of sign language, and will help pique their interest in using it. Many times, children who learn sign language in a classroom setting go home and teach their parents and siblings the language, and this facilitates its usage in the home.

CASE STUDY: JILL TULLY

Sign to Me, Sing to Me
32 Sargent Street
Melrose, Maine 02176
(781) 710-3672
jilltully@comcast.net

Jill Tully is a certified teacher of moderate special needs/elementary education. When she was teaching in a language-based special needs classroom at the primary level, she learned basic ASL because one of her students was still mostly non-verbal at the age of 5. Later, she began to integrate sign language into her elementary school classroom. Today, she teaches baby sign language classes.

I used sign language to foster communication with the non-verbal student in my class, as well as encouraged her to use language to let us know her needs and wants. We ended up using it with all of the students as they all could benefit from it. When I taught a general education kindergarten class another year, I continued to integrate sign language into our classroom routines and management.

I am a certified teacher with bachelor's degrees in elementary and special needs education, and a Master of Education degree in curriculum and instruction/special needs — all from Boston College. I took ASL training classes offered through my school district when I was teaching in order to learn basic signs to use in my classroom. I continue to learn new ASL vocabulary and am hoping to start an online course to become more fluent in true ASL. I am also a Level 1 certified presenter through Sign2Me.

Using signs with special-needs children (and actually all children) is a wonderful asset to any program. All children are visual learners, and too much auditory stimulation throughout the day can overwhelm them. Using ASL gives them a chance to receive instruction and directions from teachers and parents without using too many confusing words, which can be too much for them to take in and comprehend at times. Because

I was an elementary/special needs teacher before, I have extensive experience with teaching early literacy. This is a benefit when I am teaching preschoolclasses: I can tie in literacy and phonics activities as part of my lesson.

Ways to integrate sign into the classroom:

Communicate to the class while walking in the hallway. Sign "quiet," "good job," and "no touch."

Use sign language to allow children to still participate when it is someone else's turn. For example, if it is one child's turn to report the weather for the calendar, the other children can sign what they think it is.

Use sign language during for classroom management. Sign "look at me," "quiet," "stop," "nice work," "stand up," and "sit down." These signs allow a teacher to redirect students without interrupting the lesson.

I am currently a stay-at-home mom, a tutor for grades kindergarten through eighth, and an infant and child sign language teacher. I use many signs in my tutoring to learn sight words and teach letter names/ sounds and concepts.

In my infant/child sign language classes, children learn how to communicate basic needs to their parents and caregivers. They learn how to use ASL signs to share their experiences and interests, how to use signs to enhance their play, and how to make concrete to abstract connections, which in turn helps to foster learning and enhance literacy skills.

I also conduct training for parents and educators to help them learn basic ASL signs and how (and why) to implement using sign in their home or center. There have been so many wonderful moments with my students, and I especially love it when parents and teachers comment to me how much using sign has enhanced their family life/classroom environment. I also work part-time at a retail store at a mall, and there have been a few instances where I have been able to use the basic ASL that I know to communicate with a deaf customer, which has inspired me to try to become more fluent in sign language.

Using Sign Language in the Classroom

It is important to point out to your students that ASL is not English and is, in fact, its own language. Otherwise, children may see sign language as fun and something to do with their hands, but may not recognize it as a language because it is not spoken. The following are some tips for using ASL in the classroom:

- If you are in a preschool setting, you may begin to use sign language with the "letter of the day." If you are teaching the letter "A," you will want to teach the sign for the letter, as well as for other words that may be part of your lesson that day, such as "apple," "aunt," and "alligator."

- When you teach numbers, make the signs for all the numbers you are teaching. A fun lesson would be teaching students to sign the numbers 1 to 10 in the proper order.

- If your students are learning basic math, write a problem on the board and ask that when students raise hands to say the answer, they also sign it.

- If you are using sign language in a classroom where students are learning to read, every time you introduce a "sight word," make the sign for the word to your students.

- When students are already reading, ask them to sign the main words in a passage being read aloud by the teacher in the classroom.

Meanwhile, if you are a parent who used this book to teach your baby sign language and now want to teach your students in a classroom setting, you will need to remember that the same rules apply to teaching a class sign language as those for teaching your newborn. They are:

- Use repetition. Make the same signs over and over again.

- Make eye contact.

- Use body language.

- Show relevant signs.

- Reword the students for signing properly.

- Always say the words when you sign them.

> **Tip:**
>
> "Set a specific timeframe for teaching students sign language. For example, it is important to know how long a child can focus, and how many classes or weeks one should continue. I have a 3-year-old student and, after 40 minutes, his attention is gone. Focus on the age of the children and their individual abilities"
>
> — Heather M. Kendel, founder/executive director of ASL Advocates

20 Lesson Plans for Teaching Sign Language in Elementary School Classrooms

If you teach elementary school and want to use sign language in your classroom, it will facilitate understanding and communication, and enhance learning and literacy. With students in pre-kindergarten to fifth grade, there are several ways to do so. The following are 20 lessons plans that can help teachers integrate sign language into the classroom:

Lesson plan No. 1: Sign with storytelling

When you can introduce this: Preschool to third grade.

What you will need: A classic children's story or book, for example, "The Three Little Pigs."

How it is done:

1. Read the children's book to the class, then act out the book with body movements and gestures. At the same time, incorporate sign language into these actions. For example, you might hold your breath and blow it out at the point when the wolf wants to blow down one of the pig's house.

2. While you are doing this, make the signs for "blow," "down," and "house."

How it helps: This helps students learn about storytelling and how it is a natural part of deaf culture. It helps them learn that stories can be told by other means than spoken words.

Lesson plan No. 2: Play "May I?"

When you can introduce this: At the beginning of the semester in any grade.

What you will need: An open space in a classroom or outside in a schoolyard.

How it is done: Students will be asked to hop, jump, or walk a certain number of steps. The teacher should proceed this way:

1. Line up the students in a row.

2. When it is each student's turn, he or she will need to make the signs for "may" and "I."

3. Next, give each student a number that is signed and an action. For example, you may sign the word "hop" and the number 3, which would mean Jane should hop three times.

4. Do this for each student until someone reaches the finish line.

How it helps: This exercise shows students how to communicate in ASL. It shows them that sign language is another way to communicate, and one that can be effective.

Lesson plan No. 3: Learning feeling signs

When you can introduce this: In the younger grades to help children learn how to express their feelings.

What you will need: You will have taught the basic needs and feeling signs to the class, and have been using them daily for at least a week.

How it is done: This exercise is best done at circle time.

1. Tell each student to act out a feeling.

2. Give examples of feelings, such as sad, made, glad, excited, and angry.

3. Ask one child to act out a feeling, such as being happy.

4. The teacher then asks the students to guess what feelings the student is conveying.

5. The student should not answer, but make the sign for the feeling.

6. Give each student a turn to both act out a feeling, as well as make a guess with ASL about another student's characterization of the feeling.

How it helps: This exercise allows students to recognize feelings and use sign language to express these feelings. As noted in previous chapters, these signs could be helpful between parents and children if a child is suddenly scared. In a classroom situation, if a bully is taunting a child, and she is too afraid to tell the teacher verbally about the situation, she may choose to open up to the teacher via sign language.

Lesson plan No. 4: Create "sign time"

When you can introduce this: After the children have learned some basic sign language. Have sign time at least three times a week for 30 minutes to an hour. The time may depend on the age of the students. Younger children may have shorter attention spans.

What you will need: Various classroom materials.

How it is done: Designate a sign time of the day. It can be every day right before lunch, or it can be three times a week after recess. Once it is announced that it is "sign time," continue your regular lesson, but add sign language to it. Students should be told that all speaking at this time should be accompanied with signs. So if the teacher is teaching math, each number should be signed, and said as well. See the following example:

1. If you are teaching basic math, write a problem on the board, such as 1 + 1 = 2.

2. Say the words for the number, and "plus" and "equals," and make the sign as you say it.

3. Write your next problem on the board: 2 + 2 = ?

4. Ask the students to raise their hands, and when they answer, it should be spoken in words and signed in ASL.

How it helps: Be sure to have sign time with different subjects throughout the course of the year. This will help students broaden their ASL vocabulary. Regular signing periods also help students grow in their sign language abilities and help them gain confidence in using sign language as a second language.

Lesson plan No. 5: Learn signs for family members

When you can introduce this: In preschool or kindergarten.

What you will need: Dolls and a dollhouse.

How it is done: Show the students a dollhouse with various figures or dolls that represent members of the family. Introduce the doll by using names. For example:

1. Say, "This is Dad" as you hold up a male doll.

2. Make the sign for "Dad."

3. Repeat this with each doll and try to cover all possible immediate family members, including parents, grandparents, and siblings.

4. When you repeat the exercise, add more family members, such as cousins, aunts, and uncles.

How it helps: This exercise allows younger children to learn the meaning behind the signs as well as learn signs for the people in their lives.

Lesson plan No. 6: Practice feeling signs

When you can introduce this: After you have introduced feeling signs and words with them in the classroom. *See lesson No. 3 first.*

What you will need: Magazines.

How it is done:

1. Spread out magazines on your students' desks or tables.

2. Ask them to find three to four pictures of people.

3. Allow them to paste the pictures on a white piece of writing paper.

4. Call each student up in front of the classroom, and ask him or her to illustrate in sign language the emotion they think the person in the picture is feeling.

5. Once they have illustrated the sign, you can ask them to say the word for the sign, as well as express verbally why they think the person is feeling this particular way.

How it helps: This exercise reinforces the usage of feeling signs and allows students to learn about emotions and how they are expressed.

Lesson plan No. 7: Teach proper behavior through sign language

When you can introduce this: Any elementary grade and during any lesson.

What you will need: Another teacher to act out situations with you. This can perhaps be the assistant teacher who is often required in a preschool or kindergarten classroom. If another teacher is not available, a well-behaved student can be chosen from your class or from a higher grade classroom to participate in the exercise.

How it is done:

1. Teach the children the signs for the words "right" and "wrong."

2. Ask another teacher, an adult, or older student to roleplay with you.

3. Act out three to four situations that include proper or improper classroom behavior. Examples: Sit with the other "actor" in front of a table of blocks. Take one of the blocks out of the other actor's hands. Another situation might be the opposite scenario: Have one actor open his or her lunch to see if there is an apple in the bag. The other actor does not have a lunch bag. Therefore, one actor gives the other an apple.

4. After each scenario is played out, the students should be asked to raise their hands to recognize if there is something right or wrong with the situation.

5. They children should be asked to make either the sign for "right" or "wrong" when responding.

How it helps: This exercise allows children to recognize proper and improper behaviors and helps teach them the meaning between right and wrong. By acting out the meaning behind these words, the students are not only learning signs, but also what the signs truly mean.

Lesson plan No. 8: Reinforcing memorization through sign

When you can introduce this: This should be introduced to children who have become somewhat familiar with signing. It can be introduced at the end of the year in a preschool or kindergarten classroom, or perhaps early on in the year to a first-grade class that received ASL instruction in the year prior.

What you will need: To teach them how to play "going on a picnic."

How it is done: If you do not remember this fun childhood game, here are the steps to follow:

1. Have the students sit in a circle.

2. Ask the first child to say this phrase "I am going on a picnic and I am going to bring…"

3. Have the student choose one item to bring that begins with the letter "A." For example, one student may say, "I am going on a picnic, and I am going to bring an apple."

4. When the student says the word "apple," she should also make the sign for it.

5. The next student would say, "I am going on a picnic, and I am going to bring an apple." Make the sign for "apple," then add an item that begins with "B," such as banana. He would make the sign for "banana."

6. Repeat this with each student or until you get to the letter "Z."

How it helps: This allows students to memorize items through the use of ASL. Because sign language is visual, it will help students remember and memorize everything from a phone number to schoolwork.

Lesson plan No. 9: Play "What's in the box?"

When you can introduce this: This can be used in any grade, but needs to be used with age-appropriate items. For example, use stuffed animals, cars, and boats for preschoolers. For third-graders, use CDs or a computer mouse.

What you will need: One item for each student in the class, and a large bin.

How it is done: Put all the items in the bin (a lot of these items can be found throughout the classroom). Ask each student to take a turn closing his or her eyes and looking at the items in the bin:

1. When the student picks out an item, he should first guess what it is before he opens his eyes.

2. When he has made a guess, he should verbalize it as well as sign it.

How it helps: This game allows students to use their sense of touch to identify an object and then describe it via the visual image. For older students, you may use a blindfold and ask that they not only name the item, but also describe it in sign language through their sense of touch before the item is revealed.

Lesson plan No. 10: Teach reading skills through sign language

When you can introduce this: In kindergarten.

What you will need: Sight words written or typed on pieces of paper, and a basket.

How it is done:

1. Mix up sight words that are age-appropriate for the students in the class and put them in basket.

2. Ask each student to pick out a word, and read it aloud. After the first student reads it aloud, she also makes the sign for the word. This will help the students learn to read.

3. If you make the sign for a word, they will begin to use the image of the visual sign in their minds to remember the word when they read it.

How it helps: This exercise helps students understand how to read and helps them think visually. Remember, sign language is based on visual signs that can help students explain parts of their brain that they would not otherwise use if they were not forced to think visually.

Lesson plan No. 11: Establish signing centers

When you can introduce this: In preschool or early elementary school classes with playtime centers, such as the library, housekeeping, or blocks.

What you will need: A classroom divided into different centers.

How it is done:

1. Each week there will be a designated "signing center," which means that when communicating in the center, some form of sign language should be used along with verbal words.

2. For example, if Ashley and Ben are playing housekeeping, Ashley might be pretending to cook a hot dog. She may say to Ben, "I

am cooking a hot dog." When she says this, she should also make the sign for cook and hot dog.

How it helps: This will allow the students to learn to converse in sign language. It will help them understand that this is, in fact, a language, even though it is visual. The same signing centers can be set up where there are no spoken words, and the children are instructed to communicate strictly via sign language.

Lesson plan No. 12: Signing games to teach signing vocabulary

When you can introduce this: In first grade and above.

What you will need: Flashcards or pictures pasted on index cards.

How it is done: Divide the students into two teams. The team that produces the largest signing vocabulary wins. Play the game this way:

1. Ask the students to stand in two straight lines facing each other.

2. The first two students in line should toss a coin to see who will go first.

3. Display a photo on a flashcard, for example, a picture of a monkey.

4. The student who wins the coin toss needs to make the sign for "monkey." If she does not know it, she can get help from her teammates.

5. Once she makes the sign correctly, she can go to other end of the line and wait for her next turn.

6. The team with the right answer earns one point.

7. However, if no one on the team could make the proper sign, the other team is allowed to try. If they get it correct, they score one point.

8. Next turn is granted to the first member of the opposing team.

9. The game is played until each student has had at least two turns making a sign.

10. The team with the highest score wins.

11. Reward the entire class for their participation and explain that even if the sign was wrong, it is good to have made an attempt.

How it helps: This helps students increase their signing vocabulary and encourages them to learn more.

Lesson plan No. 13: Learn food signs

When you can introduce this: During lunch in any grade.

What you will need: To extend lunch by 15 minutes to allow the children to complete the exercise and finish their lunches.

How it is done:

1. Go around the table and ask the kids to say and sign what is in their lunchboxes. If a student does not know a particular sign (for example, the sign for turkey), model it for her, and ask students to make that sign.

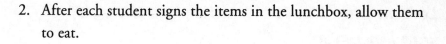

2. After each student signs the items in the lunchbox, allow them to eat.

How it helps: This exercise teaches food signs and is an opportunity to model an array of signs for your students. It can also be completed during circle time where you ask each student to name one item in his or her refrigerator at home, and make the sign for that item. When applying the exercise in this manner, you also tap into the students' visual memory skills.

Lesson plan No. 14: Use sign language while singing

When you can introduce this: Teach signs to children as part of their music program.

What you will need: Children's songs.

How it is done:

1. Choose songs the children will regularly rehearse. After you have taught the songs, also teach the signs for the key words in the songs.

2. Every time the song is practiced, make sure the students make the accompanying signs. It is common for schools to do this for songs that will be performed at a concert or graduation.

How it helps: This will allow the students to display their signing abilities to an audience that consists of their teacher, parents, and other family members. It will also spread the word that ASL is a language used to communicate words. At some point in a song, such as the chorus, it is helpful if the students stop singing the words to the song and just sign them. This will convey that they are communicating with the audience through another language.

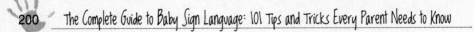

Lesson plan No. 15: Teach colors though sign language

When you can introduce this: Preschool.

What you will need: Paints and an easel.

How it is done:

1. Ask each student to come up to the easel individually and choose a color.

2. Ask the student to paint something on the canvas.

3. After a student puts down his brush, show the class the sign for the color.

4. Ask the class to perform the sign.

5. Once all the primary colors have been used, ask the students to mix two colors to make another. For example, red and blue make purple.

6. Make the signs for each color used, as well as the color created.

7. Ask the class to make the signs.

8. Always have them say the words while they are making the signs. This will help them remember at a young age what the colors are, as well as the signs for them.

How it helps: This exercise teachers colors and the signs for colors in a fun, interactive way that allows students to be creative and learn at the same time.

Lesson plan No. 16: Play bingo using words and sign

When you can introduce this: First grade.

What you will need: A bingo board made with words for each student. Some school supply stores carry these, but they can easily be made at home using simple words, such as "cat," "hat," "bat," "in," "the," and "Mom."

How it is done:

1. Give each student a bingo board.

2. As the teacher, you are the bingo caller.

3. As you pick out a word, sign it and say it to the class.

4. The class will then mimic the sign and find it on their boards.

5. Continue this until a student calls bingo. When he does, make sure he signs the words when he says it.

How it helps: This allows students to broaden both their vocabulary and signing abilities. You can play this game in the classroom once a month and use different boards where the words on the board get more challenging. The children also are using a visual means to aid in their memory of how the words are spelled.

Lesson plan No. 17: Introduce fingerspelling through the name game

When you can introduce this: Once students are familiar with basic signs.

What you will need: An alphabet chart.

How it is done:

1. Have a letter of the day each school day where you introduce a new letter. Illustrate the sign for the letter and use it in words throughout the day.

2. By the end of the day, you should have repeated the sign for the letter at least 15 times, and all your students should have practiced it with you.

How it helps: Learning fingerspelling can help your students with their spelling abilities. When you teach signs for a new letter in a day, make sure your students repeat letters already learned. Start to spell three-letter words and progress to four-letter words. This will help build signing and spelling confidence.

Lesson plan No. 18: Use fingerspelling to learn new vocabulary words

When you can introduce this: When children are learning to spell new words in any grade.

What you will need: A vocabulary list.

How it is done: Write new words that your students will need to learn to spell on the blackboard. Read the words, then fingerspell them. After you fingerspell each word, have the students mimic you. Although you may not be able to see if every student is fingerspelling the words correctly, use repetition to have them get it right. A good way to do this is go around the room and have them come up with a sentence using the word they should fingerspell. Example:

1. Assign the word "finger."

2. Write the word on the chalkboard and say it, then sign it.

3. Have the student learn how to fingerspell the word.

4. Go around the classroom, and ask that each student come up with a sentence using the word "finger."

5. When each student says the word, have him or her fingerspell it.

How it helps: When children learn to spell and use fingerspelling, they have a visual image for the word as they sound it out and recall how to spell it.

Lesson plan No. 19: Learn the seasons with sign

When you can introduce this: Any time and at any elementary grade.

What you will need: Pictures of seasonal items, such as hats, scarves, umbrellas, leaves, the beach, sunglasses, and bathing suits.

How it is done: Have the students come up in the front of the class one by one. Ask them to choose a photo from those in a basket. Once a child has the picture, follow these steps:

1. Ask the student to reveal the photo to the class.

2. Ask the student to say the word for the item pictured, for example, "bathing suit."

3. Model the sign for that item.

4. Have the student make the sign.

5. Ask the student what season the item belongs in.

6. When he says "summer," show that sign and have the class make it as well.

How it helps: This exercise helps students with association and learning seasons. It is also a good way to reinforce sign language skills.

Lesson plan No. 20: Learn the days of the week and months of the year with sign language

When you can introduce this: Preschool and kindergarten.

What you will need: A calendar.

How it is done:

1. Ask the children to think of their birthday month and the things associated with it.

2. Question each student about what he or she is thinking.

3. If one student says she is thinking of building a snowman for her birthday in January, show the students the month of January on the calendar, then ask them the sign for calendar.

4. Also, model the signs for "snowman" and "cold."

5. Do this also for days of the week by asking students questions pertaining to each day, such as, "What day do we have gym?"

6. When a student answers, "Tuesday," show her the day on the calendar and make the sign.

How it helps: This helps children learn the signs for days of the week and months of the year. It also broadens their sign language vocabulary.

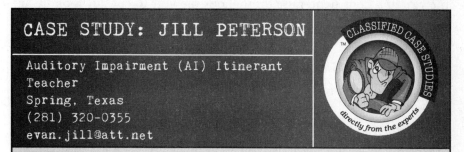

CASE STUDY: JILL PETERSON

Auditory Impairment (AI) Itinerant
Teacher
Spring, Texas
(281) 320-0355
evan.jill@att.net

CLASSIFIED CASE STUDIES
™
directly from the experts

With a college degree in deaf education from Stephen F. Austin State University in Nacogdoches, Texas, Jill Peterson used sign language in the classroom to teach students who were deaf or have hearing impairments. She currently works for the Northwest Harris County Co-op for the Deaf. She works with families of children who have been diagnosed with a hearing impairment. She believes sign language is a great tool for all elementary school teachers to integrate into the classroom.

All children and adults use "sign" during their lifetime. Everyone knows what it means when someone crooks a finger ("come here"), or when a child holds up his arms — every adult knows that means "pick me up." Sign language is a great way to ease frustrations with children.

Teachers can integrate sign language into a mainstream classroom by labeling things in the classroom with the word and the sign, sing songs in sign, teach the children signs for requests (like using the restroom), and teach them the signs for "yes" and "no" that can be used when communicating with peers and the teacher. If there is a deaf student in the class who uses an interpreter, encourage students to learn to communicate with the hearing-impaired student.

Sign Language as a Classroom Management Tool

In addition to great benefits for learning, sign language can help curb disruptive behavior in the classroom. If students are being disruptive, you as the teacher can say "Stop doing that," and make the sign for "stop." In this way, sign language becomes an extra management tool you can use to promote harmony in a classroom setting.

Following is a list of ways teachers can incorporate sign language to help manage students. Teachers should illustrate important signs at the onset of the year and consistently use throughout the year to cut down on disruptions in the classroom:

- **"Quiet":** Use this sign when students are talking when they should not be socializing.

- **"Calm down":** When you see potentially disruptive behavior igniting in the classroom, use this sign to calm the students down before the activity escalates.

- **"Good job":** This sign rewards students for a job well done and encourages a sense of pride.

- If you are teaching a lesson, ask students during class to reply in sign language. They are less likely to become distracted and more eager to answer due to the extra task that will be needed to complete the answer.

- If a child needs to use the bathroom during quiet time, instead of disrupting the other students, she can make the sign for "potty" or "toilet" and the teacher can take her without waking the other children.

- **An example for an elementary school classroom:** When students are taking a test and a student has a question, he or she can ask the teacher through the use of sign language, and the teacher can answer in sign language.

ASL Syntax and Grammar

Teachers can use ASL grammar and syntax to show how sign language is different from English. ASL syntax consists of word order combinations that basically follows a "subject, verb, object" order. In many cases, there is flexibility in ASL word order. For example, within a noun phrase, the word order is noun-number and noun-adjective. ASL syntax lacks linkage to a verb. For example, "My feet are cold" is signed "My feet cold;" "My name is Tracey" is signed "Name my T-R-A-C-E-Y."

In addition, ASL communication centers on topics. The topic of the sentence is mentioned first and is discussed in the main clause, which also includes background information. For example, in ASL, you would sign, "That cat, I just adore him." The topic is the cat, and the meaning you want to convey about the cat follows it in ASL.

ASL also uses "time-sequenced ordering," which means occurrences are signed in the order in which they occurred. For example, for "I missed work yesterday because I woke up with a fever in the middle of the night," you would sign: "Middle of the night, fever, work missed yesterday for me." However, when signing a story, you can chose the order in which you want to sequence the events. In other words, you can choose the time sequencing that will make the most sense in the particular story you are telling. When it comes to adjectives, ASL usually places adjectives after nouns. Numbers are also placed after a noun. For example, if you were to speak the sentence, "I have a spotted cat," you would sign "Cat spotted I have," However, adverbs are often placed before verbs. For example, if you were to say "I drive my car speedily to work," you would sign, "Car I speed to work." It is important to note that teachers who use sign language in the classroom do not have to be fluent in ASL. You can teach yourself the signs you need to know. If you use it regularly in your classroom, it will become more natural and easier as you continue. As you grow in your confidence in using ASL, so will your students. If you are fluent, do not require that your students become fluent. Show them signs and make this a fun and anticipated part of their learning.

Chapter Thirteen

Parents' Point of View/ Stories That Inspire

Though this book has armed you with all you need to know to teach your child sign language and more, it is important to let you know that these tips really work. In this chapter, you will find short anecdotal stories that will illustrate how parents have taught their children sign language and learned from them as well. Many of these stories will inspire you to continue along this path of learning sign language with your child. When you get discouraged, read some of these delightful success stories from parents across the country who are using sign language with their children.

Parent Success Stories

Request for a midnight snack

Dawn Babb Prochovnic thoroughly enjoyed teaching her children to sign. She signed to her daughter, Katia, since she was 4 months old, and she began to respond through sign language at the age of 7 months. One day she woke up crying in the middle of the night. When Dawn and her husband, Sam, went into Katia's room to see what was wrong, she emphatically signed "banana." The Prochovnics would never have imagined that she wanted a banana in the middle of the night. She got her banana and was soon happy and went back to sleep.

The Prochovnics started signing with their son, Nikko, from the day he was born. The very first time Katia met her new baby brother, she got down close to him, took his little fists into her hands, and tapped them together gently as if to sign "more. She said to him, "Hi, little brother. I'm going to teach you how to sign."

Creating a trilingual child through sign

Rebekah and Nate Jorgensen of Roseville, Minnesota, wanted to use sign language with their daughter Natali in order to raise her to be trilingual in German, English, and ASL. Because Nate does not speak German, some of the signs were easier for him to learn than the German words. Rebekah admits to being concerned that by teaching her daughter two verbal languages, spoken words might come later rather than sooner. But she figured the signing would help her words come sooner.

Natali signed before she could talk. She also had mastered about a dozen signs before she spoke more than "ma ma" and "pa pa." She learned all the basic needs signs, so it helped her parents figure out what she needed when she got fussy.

The sign language helped better explain words that sounded the same from the two languages to Natali. For example, in German, the word for "cheese" is "käse," and the word for "cookie" or "cracker" is "kekse." They sound very similar, so having Natali learn the signs for them helped her differentiate between the two words and convey to her parents what she wanted.

Today, Natali's signing skills are advanced. She picks up signs that her parents do not yet know from babysitters and some of the nursery volunteers at their church.

Signing sisters

Wendy Cohen of Northridge, California, did not know a word of sign language before she started using it with her two daughters, Hannah, now 17, and Sadie, 11. So she bought a book and taught herself sign language. In 1993, before signing with a preverbal hearing baby was popular, Wendy set out to teach her children how to communicate before they could talk.

Her daughters learned the ASL alphabet, and through the years, both girls have greatly increased their sign language vocabularies. When Sadie's fifth-grade teacher began using sign language in the classroom, Sadie found some people other than her immediate family to converse with via sign language. At home, the Cohens use sign language every day. When the girls were young, Wendy found sign language to be a handy tool by which her daughters could convey their feelings of being overwhelmed when in a group of friends, or if they felt afraid in a group situation. In these situations, the Cohen sisters would fingerspell out a word or phrase like "help" or "I'm afraid." That way, someone could come to the rescue without their feeling shy or embarrassed to speak out directly.

Wendy was recently with her daughters in a restaurant in Malibu, where there were people using sign language. The girls approached them and signed a little of what they knew. The signers wore a look of surprise on their faces because these two hearing children knew sign language. However, Wendy's most fond sign language memory is when Sadie was 4 years old and Hannah was 10. They both walked right up to a person, totally uninhibited, and spelled out "hello" and "What is your name?" Wendy just sat back and nodded.

Signing families

Jennifer Simpson of West Granby, Connecticut, began signing with her daughters Emma and Katie, who are 7-year-old twins, when they were about 7 months old. Her son Bennett, now age 5, was exposed to sign from birth, and Graham, who is now 1 year old, was signed to at about 10 months of age.

The kids all began signing at about 11 months, with the earliest spoken words soon to follow. All of Jennifer's children were verbal by 18 months, but they still used their signs to support their developing spoken language. However, she says their usage of ASL decreased when they were 2 or 3 years old. But at about age 3, the twins again became interested in sign language. They wanted to learn the sign language alphabet.

Today, the Simpsons continue to use signing in different aspects of their lives. In large groups or noisy situations, they will use sign language to convey simple ideas, such as "five more minutes," "It is time to go," "Do you need to go to the ladies' room?" or "Say please." In addition, they make games out of fingerspelling words to pass the time in waiting rooms and restaurants. However, the Simpson kids most enjoy learning to sign parts of their favorite songs.

Perhaps her most fond memory, said Jennifer, is when the twins were about 18 months old and she was taking a video of them playing with their toys. When an adult told them to "say cheese for the camera" they instead looked up, smiled, and made the sign for "cheese."

Learning the "hurt" sign

When Cindy Santa Ana's daughter was about 18 months old, she was sick with a cold. She was very fussy and did not seem to be herself but was not exhibiting any symptoms except for a runny nose and crankiness. After much prodding from her mother about what was wrong, she finally signed "hurt" at her throat. Cindy took her to the doctor, and to her surprise ,she had strep throat. In this case, sign language helped her daughter get the medical attention she needed.

First signs

Katherine Joyce Huang of Cambridge, Massachusetts, started signing with her son, Julian, when he was about 7 months old. He is now 20 months old and makes 35 to 40 signs. However, his first sign was not about any basic needs. Instead, he made his first sign when he was about 10 months, and it pertained to his best friend — the family dog. The family had an enormous Great Pyrenees Mountain dog. Julian pointed to it, made an "eh?" sound, and made the sign for dog. He likely wanted to let his mother know the dog was something that he liked.

Soon after, Julian began signing all the words he had watched his family make since birth so diligently. He quickly began making one or two new signs per week once he started signing. Within a few weeks, he was "compound signing" all sorts of interesting things. One day, Katherine was watching an episode of Oprah in which she had her new puppy on the show. Julian, at about 13 months old, ran up to the television, pointed to the puppy, and signed "dog" and "baby."

More music?

Signing parents Kelly and Casey Kohen of Davis, California, started signing with their son, Corey, now 22 months old, at birth. Kelly fondly recalls his enthusiasm about using the sign for "more." It seemed as if he suddenly wanted more of everything from that point on. But one time in particular stands out in her memory. The family was playing music, and Corey was dancing around the room. Each time the music stopped, he would sign "more" until it came on again, then he would start dancing.

More learning the sign for "more"

New York City resident Lora Heller's sons both were taught sign language from birth. Her oldest son first signed an approximation of "I love you" when he was 6 months old. Every morning, the family exchanged signs for "Good morning, I love you." One morning, he signed "I love you" before his parents did. While this was a huge milestone at 10 months, when Lora entered his room on another occasion, "I love you" was not his first sign of the day. That morning, he signed "more music" because his mobile on his crib had stopped playing familiar tunes.

Favorite signs

One of Kelly Kohen's favorite signs her son Corey makes is the "scared" sign. If he sees something he does not like or is afraid of, his family will know exactly what the issue is because he will use the sign to tell them. Many times, Corey's parents would find him crying, and they could not figure out why. Did he want to be held? Was he hungry? Did he need a diaper change? But now, when he makes the sign, everyone understands the feelings behind his tears, and his parents can instantly comfort him or explain that there is nothing to be afraid of to ease his fears.

Fan-tastic signing

Emily Bosak of Knightdale, North Carolina, started teaching sign language to her son, Cameron, at the age of 4 months. She soon observed him staring at her hands while they moved to make the signs. She would notice any time was signing to him that he appeared eager as he intensely watched her signs. At 6 months, he signed "Ma ma" and "Da da." But all the words that Emily was signing just were not as exciting to Cameron as those that were most relevant to his world. At 8 months old, Emily noticed that he liked to look up at ceiling fans and lights, so she began signing those words to him. Almost immediately, he picked up the signs for "fan" and "light." Soon after, he definitely became very interested in talking about bugs. For that reason, she taught him the signs for all the bugs and everything else in his world that he really liked.

Perceptive signing

Beth Blair of Oro Valley, Arizona, recalls her fondest sign language-related memory as when she and her husband were sitting in a Mexican restaurant enjoying a meal when her son, Jeb, started signing "cow." They looked at each other, thinking he was surely confused. But on a counter was a statue of a cow, and the 1-year-old Jeb apparently wanted to let his parents know it caught his eye.

When Beth was in the hospital having her second child, a baby girl they named Madeline, her parents took him to a toy store for some last-minute baby gifts. Jeb started pointing to a big pink poodle stuffed animal and looked at his grandparents while signing "baby." He immediately made the association of pink and his new baby sister. Beth thinks this may have been the result of all of the pink gifts the family received. Of course, the poodle ended up being a gift from Jeb to Madeline. To this day, Jeb wants "nothing to do with the color pink, but is happy to pass anything pink along to his little sister," Beth said.

Easing frustration

Julie Russell of Quincy, Maine, started signing with her son, Atticus, now 8 years old, when he was about 10 months old. His first three signs were "more" "eat," and "drink." He was probably 10 to 11 months when he started using sign language to communicate with his family. An "easy baby" according to Julie, Atticus had few tantrums as a baby, and his parents attribute that to his early signing abilities. Because he could convey through sign language that he was hungry, thirsty, needed more of something, or wanted to get down from his high chair, he was a very happy baby. Julie said that Atticus is a great reader and spoke early. She attributes some of this to signing.

Sign approximations

Pierre Bastien of Long Island City, New York, started signing with his son, Luc, who is now almost 2 years old, at the age of 1. Pierre was amazed at how Luc seemed to understand the value of signing almost immediately after being exposed to it. Though not all his signs were perfect, his parents understood his early signing abilities just like a parent would understand their own child's verbal "baby speak" well.

Good advice

Bronx, New York-resident Réal Hamilton-Romeo started signing with her daughter, Faren, now age 3, when she started clapping at approximately 7 months old. Every time she clapped, Réal would ask if she was hungry, sleepy, or thirsty, and she would say and sign it to Faren. Réal started signing basic signs to her daughter, and it was not long before she began to grasp these concepts with ease. Even when she started speaking, she would sign simultaneously.

For this reason, Réal recommends starting to teach a child sign language as early a possible, and said the moment a child begins to wave or clap is when she is ready to learn to sign because she now has the ability to make hand gestures that will allow her to communicate with you.

Réal says her caregiver helped reinforce the signing, as she had a child 6 months older than Faren, whom she communicated with via sign language. Réal says she feels that Faren grasped signing, talking, and other milestones a lot faster than the caregiver's daughter. Although Faren does not use sign language as much today as she did as a baby, today she uses it to get her point across. If she asks Réal for something to eat or drink multiple times and Réal does not respond, Faren will often say, "Do you hear me?" Then she will sign as a last resort.

Learning to sign

Rebekah Jorgensen, who taught her daughter, Natali, sign language to help her family become bilingual in German and English, has a severely autistic and very non-verbal cousin, and a cousin who is mentally handicapped and hard-of-hearing. Both of them use ASL to communicate. Although the Jorgensens do not see these cousins often, as they live a12-hour drive away, she recalls her daughter's first visit with them. At the age of 1, Natali watched intently as her cousins would sign to each other. Then she would try to imitate their signs. The cousins would see her signing and try to sign back to her. Though she was unclear of the meanings, she knew they meant something and it ignited her eagerness to learn sign language.

Signing in deaf households

William Millios of Frederick, Maryland, is deaf. He attended high school at a school for the deaf and attended Gallaudet University. He can, however, speak "normally," and can communicate by speech and hearing with other people. He is fluent in ASL. He started signing with his daughter, Katie, now 13 years old, when she was about 5 months old, and with his son, Billy, now age 12, when he was about 7 months old. William and his wife, Doris, believed Katie had normal hearing, but later found out she had a moderate hearing loss.

Katie tested at a 12th-grade reading level in the fifth and sixth grade. Billy, who is just out of sixth grade, also tested at the 12th-grade reading comprehension level. William attributes much of this success to signing. One of his favorite stories occurred when Katie was about 1 year old and her favorite food was tomatoes. Every night, she would get in her high chair and start signing, "Tomato, tomato." If there were no tomatoes, then she would become upset. William remembers having to drive to the store several times to get tomatoes at the last minute.

Baby ASL interpreters

Sharon Heywood of Lakeville, Minnesota, used sign language with all four of her children, who range in age from 9 to 17. At 9 months old, her third child, Matthew, now 11, was diagnosed with severe-to-profound hearing loss. The family had been signing to Matthew since birth, and his siblings were becoming well-versed in ASL.

When Sharon's daughter Grace, who is now 9 years old, was 3 years old and her deaf brother was about 6, she was interpreting a conversation that was being had for him; at this young age, she signed every word for him.

Sign substitutes

After initiating sign language communication with Brayden (now 2) at 6 months old, Monika Mira of Eleele, Hawaii, soon found herself having sign language conversations with her 10-month-old son.

By 17 months, he knew about 65 signs and, by 19 months, he had mastered 100 signs. He has chosen not to use some signs shown to him by his parents. Now that he is speaking, he uses sign language less. If he is not getting what he wants or begins to get frustrated with trying to communicate, he will add the signs back in, said Monika. The family still uses as many signs as possible each day to continue to foster Brayden's sign language abilities. His mother said the cutest thing is when he substitutes a sign for something he does not know the word or sign for, but is similar. An example of this occurred when he signed "knife" for "scissors," and "bicycle" for "motorcycle."

A parent's story

By the time Laura Berg's daughter was 10 months old, she knew almost a dozen signs, mainly those for her favorite foods. Laura described the scenario: "One day, she was eating cereal and signing 'more.' I would give her more, and she would throw them on the floor and sign 'more' again. I said to her, 'Then you do not want more; what do you want?' She looked at me and signed 'more cheese,'" recalled Laura, the founder of My Smart Hands. She was amazed because her daughter had put together a two-word sentence at 10 months old and there was no cheese in sight, yet her baby knew that she wanted it.

Sign Language Journal

The best way to keep track of your child's progress in his ability to learn sign language is to keep a journal. Make a point to record in your journal all progress, from new signs to learning how to fingerspell words. The journal entries do not have to be lengthy; they simply need to record the strides your child makes in his signing journey.

Use the following format to record progress on a daily, weekly, or monthly basis — or simply whenever your child reaches a signing milestone:

Date: _____

Signs your child knows (In the beginning, this will be words; as his vocabulary grows, it will become a number of signs he knows how to make):

_____

_____

_____

_____

_____

_____

_____

_____

Recent progress: _____

_____

_____

_____

_____

_____

_____

_____

_____

_____

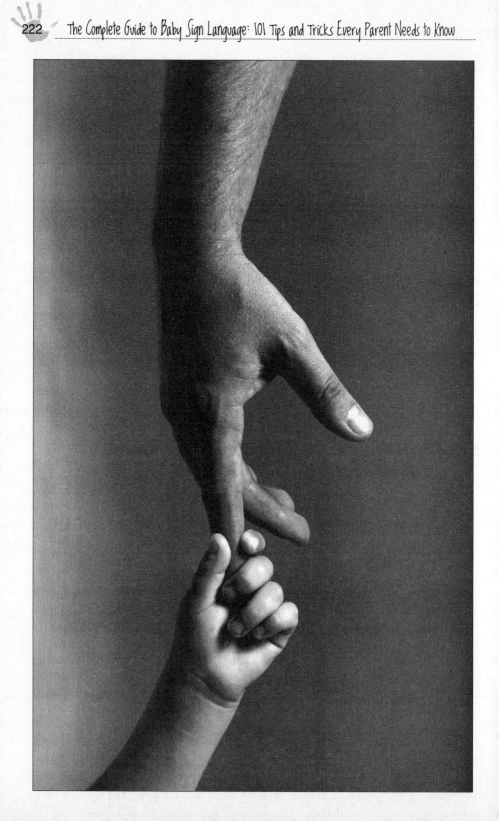

Appendix A

Sign Language Dictionary

Sign language is not only communication with your hands — it also involves appropriate facial expression, correct position of the hands, and correct movement. To get started, you need to learn which hand to use and when. Predominantly use the hand that you write with, which is known as the "dominant" hand. For example, if you write with your right hand, that is your dominant hand. Your left hand would be your non-dominant hand. These terms will be used in the explanations in this dictionary. Use your non-dominant hand only when signs are made with both hands.

Signs are often made with what is termed "handshapes," which are usually based on the letters of the alphabet or on numbers. You will see this term in the dictionary through clues such as "Use the number 5 handshape to make this sign."

Sign language also involves copying a natural motion, such as with the sign "to drink." These are noted as "iconic signs."

Now new signers are bound to make errors, whether you are an adult or a child. Practice and experience will help you remember how to sign correctly and with more ease. I will give you a hint: When you are first learning to sign, watch yourself in a mirror. This way you can see how the sign is made from two viewpoints, including what your child is viewing.

If you make a mistake, do not panic. Your child probably will not notice if the error is only made a single time. Relax, enjoy your new skill and, most importantly, help your child to communicate.

N U M B E R S

One

Two

Three

Four

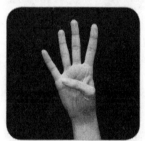

Five

Six

Seven

Eight

Nine

Ten

ALPHABET

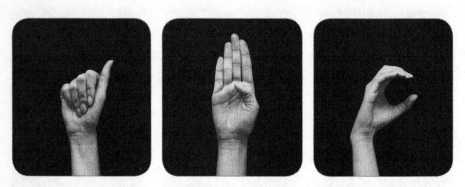

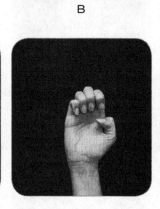

A

B

C

D

E

F

G

H

I

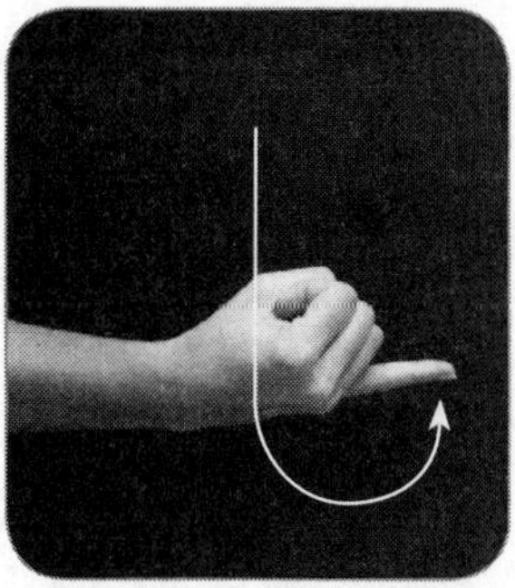

J

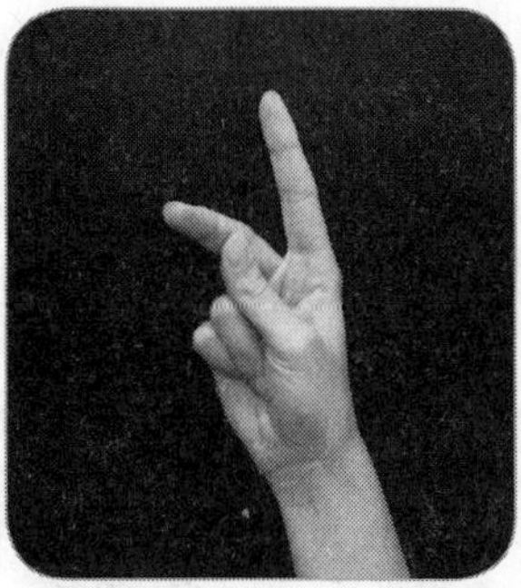

K

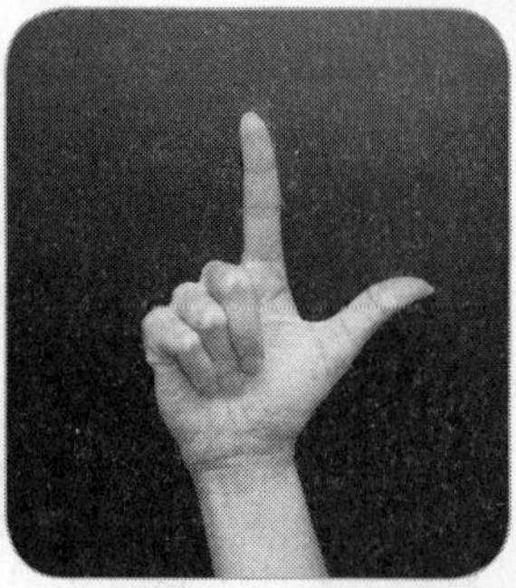

L

M

N

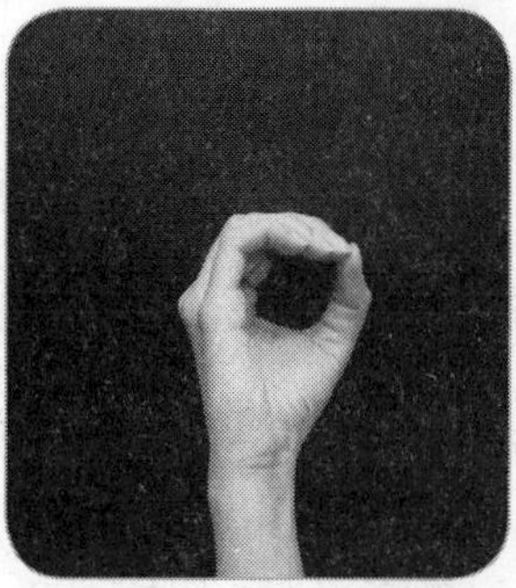

O

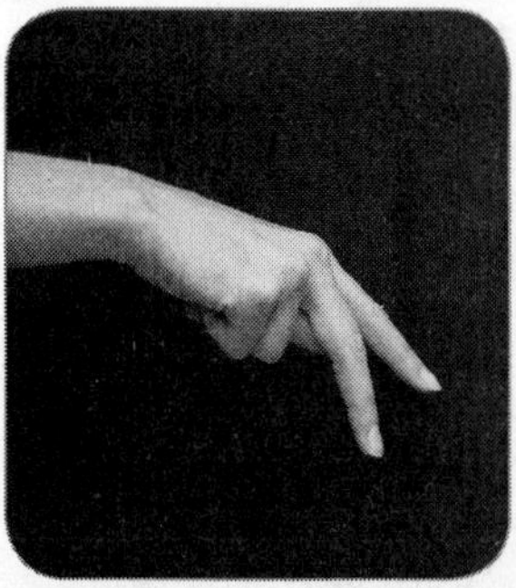

P

Q

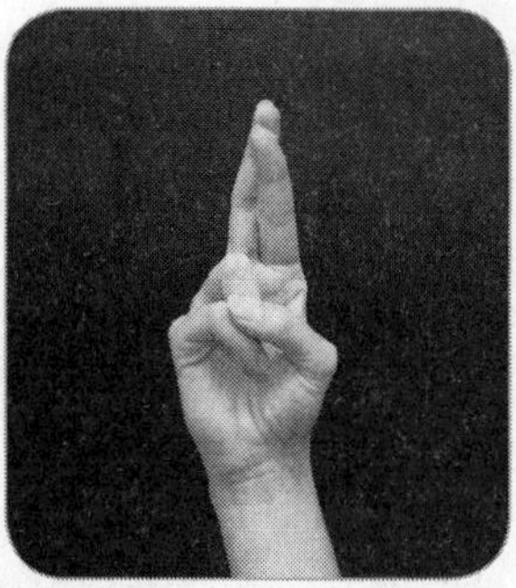

R

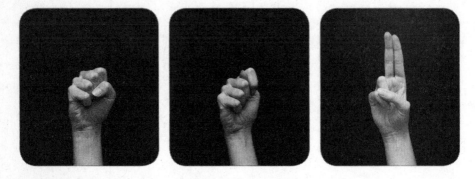

S   T   U

V   W   X

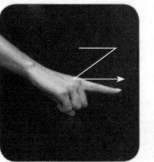

Y   Z

M O N T H S

It is easiest and most common to fingerspell the first three letters of each month of the year — except for months with five or fewer letters. Months with five or fewer letters (such as "July") are spelled out, and "September" is fingerspelled with four letters.

Signed English includes signs for each month, but most deaf people prefer to use the abbreviated spelling because this is the quickest way.

January

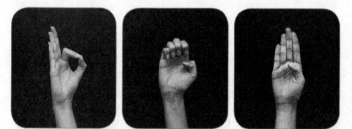

February

March

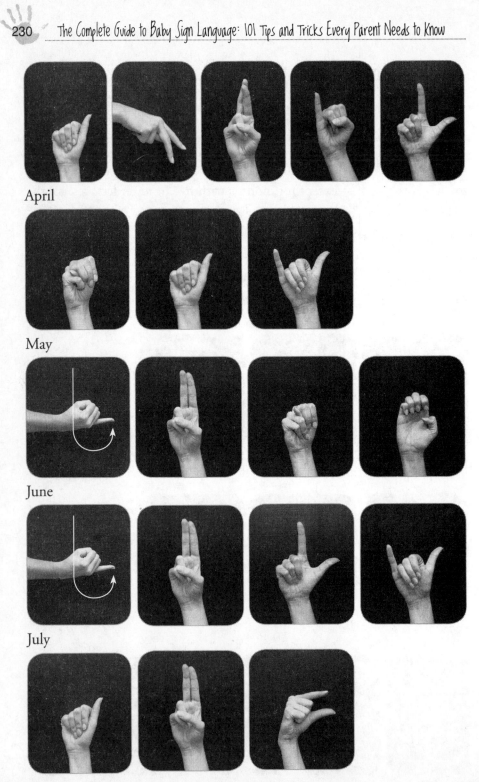

April

May

June

July

August

September

October

November

December

COMMON WORDS

- A -

Afraid:

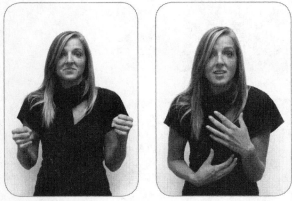

Pretend you are scared.

Apple:

Place knuckle of your index finger against your cheek above your mouth and pivot the hand back and forth.

- B -

Baby:

Pretend you are holding a baby; gently rock your arms back and forth.

Ball:

Pretend you are holding a ball. This sign can also mean "softball."

Banana:

Pretend you're peeling a banana. Start from the tip of your finger and pull down. Two to three "peels" will be fine.

Bath:

Imitate the act of holding a washcloth and scrubbing in a bathtub. Move your hands up and down from your upper- to mid-chest region.

Bird:

Make the letter "G" and place it to the right side of your mouth. Open and close your fingers twice, like a beak. This sign can also mean "chicken."

Bite:

Make your right hand "bite" your left hand. Hands will be reversed if your dominant hand is the left.

Black:

Using your dominant hand, take your index finger and slide it across your eyebrow from left to right. Reverse the motion if left is your dominant hand.

Blue:

Use the letter "B" handshape, and flip your hand back and forth at the wrist.

Book:

This is a double-motion sign. Pretend you have a book in your hands, then open and close it. The single motion from close to open means "open book." The single motion from open to close means "close your book."

Bottle:

Outline the shape of a bottle in your hands. The sign is made with the hand-shape of the letter "C." Place your dominant hand on your open non-dominant hand. Move it upward to show the height of a bottle.

- C -

Car:

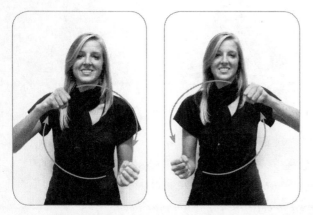

Pretend you are steering a wheel from side to side. This is also the sign for "drive."

Careful:

Make a "K" with both hands. Place right hand on top of left. Move your hand in a circular motion: forward, downward, backward, and finally upward.

Cat:

Make the handshape of the letter "F" and pretend to pull the whiskers of a cat.

Cereal:

Starting from the right side of your face, use your right hand to point across your chin. Move your hand across the front of your face and change it to an "X handsign. Change from straight to "X" a couple of times.

Cheese:

Place both hands together and rotate back and forth two to three times.

Clothes:

Take your open hand (in the shape of the number 5) and move it up and down your body twice starting at about an inch out from your upper chest. The thumb should be closest to the body when you begin the sign.

Coat:

Imitate putting on your coat.

- D -

Dad:

Make an open number 5 handshape and place on the forehead. Tap forehead gently two times.

Diaper:

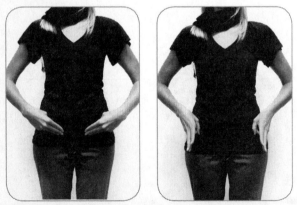

Mimic the motion of tape fasteners closing.

Dog:

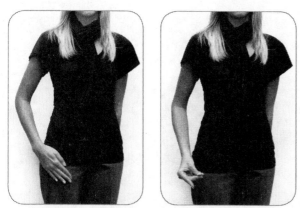

A child will simply hit the side of her thigh to imitate calling for a dog. An adult will hit his thigh and then snap his fingers.

Don't:

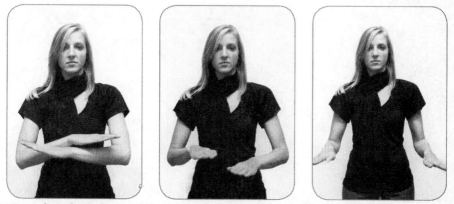

Cross hands in front of the body as shown. Do not forget to use the appropriate facial expression.

Drink:

Imitate the action of holding a cup and drinking.

- F -

Family:

Using the letter "F" handshape, start with the thumbs close to the body as demonstrated in the photo, then make a circle away from the body until the pinky fingers touch.

Feel:

Start the sign a bit lower than the chest area. Use the handshape shown (middle finger touching the upper chest) and tap two to three times in the same area.

Fine:

Using the open number 5 handshape, have the thumb touch and tap the upper chest area two times.

Finish/Over/Done:

Start with the hands raised, then quickly lower, as if flicking something off your hands.

Food/Eat:

Imitate eating something from your hands.

Friend:

Link index fingers together and then reverse. This imitates "blood brothers."

- G -

Grandfather:

Same as "Dad," but bounce the open number 5 handshape away from the forehead.

Grandmother:

Same as "Mom", but bounce the open number 5 handshape away from the chin.

Grape:

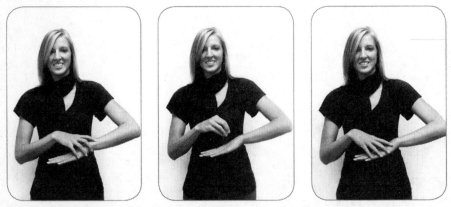

Pretend to pick a bunch of grapes, as demonstrated. Repeat sign at least one time.

Green:

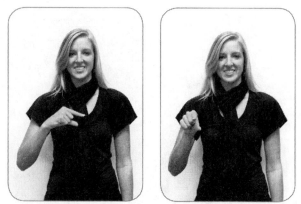

Make the handshape for the letter "G" in front of the body and twist back and forth two to three times.

- H -

Happy:

Slightly touch the open hand to the chest and move the hand in a circular motion, going away from the body and then back to the body again. The hand moves away, with the thumb always being upright.

Hat:

Take your hand and touch the top of your head once.

Hear/Listen:

Use your hand to cup your ear.

Help:

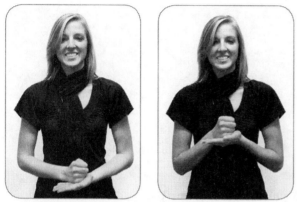

Lay the non-dominant hand flat with palm facing upward and form the dominant hand in a fist. Lay the fist on the open hand. The bottom hand "helps" the other one up.

Hot:

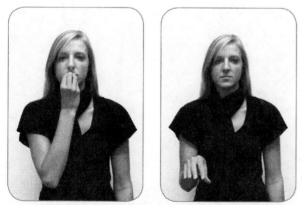

Place your hand to your mouth as demonstrated and "drop" the hand as if something were too hot to hold.

Hot Dog:

Start with the handshape for the letter "S." Have your hands open and close, going in opposing directions as if you are squeezing meat to make hot dog links.

Hungry:

Use the handshape for the letter "C." Start at the upper chest area and move toward your mid-section once.

Hurt:

A child will use both index fingers and touch them together. An adult will use the position in the left photo and twist the fingers in opposite directions.

- J -

Juice:

Take your handshape for the letter "J" and twist the pinky finger from the mouth out. You can also make this sign by combining the word for "drink" with the letter "J." As children become older, you can add another sign, such as "orange" or "apple."

- M -

Mad/Grouchy:

Using a curled/bent number 5 handshape in front of the face, mimic making an angry face. If you are mad, then you only would "scrunch" your hand a single time. "Grouchy" is more intense, but the sign is duplicated.

Milk:

Using the handshape demonstrated, squeeze twice. This mimics the milking of a cow.

Mine:

Place hand on chest to show possession.

Mom:

Place the handshape of the number 5 with the thumb touching the chin. Tap two times.

Moon:

Start with a modified handshape for letter "C," using only the thumb and index finger. Place to the side of the dominant side's eye, then move up to show that the moon rises in the sky.

More:

Use the handshape as demonstrated. It resembles putting two things together.

Music:

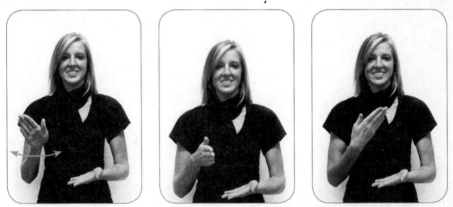

Position your non-dominant hand flat, palm facing upward. Wave your dominant hand, as shown, back and forth, as if you are keeping time with the music.

- N -

No:

Use the handshape for the number 3 and close it tightly, as demonstrated in the photos.

Nurse:

Made with the letter "N," place it on your wrist as if taking your pulse.

Off:

Place your non-dominant hand flat with palm facing downward. The dominant hand lifts off the back of the non-dominant hand.

On:

Place your non-dominant hand flat with palm facing downward. Place the dominant hand on the back of the non-dominant hand.

Orange:

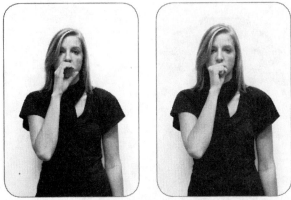

Place the handshape for the letter "O" over the chin and then squeeze. It is meant to resemble squeezing the orange (fruit).

- P -

Pacifier:

Imitate placing a pacifier to the mouth.

Pants:

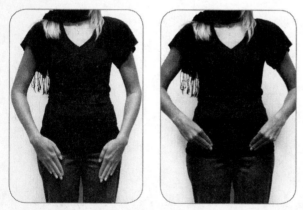

Start with your hands flat and open on the upper part of your pants area, as shown. Then pull up slightly to imitate pulling up a pair of trousers.

Play:

Make the handshape for the letter "Y" and twist the wrist two times.

Please:

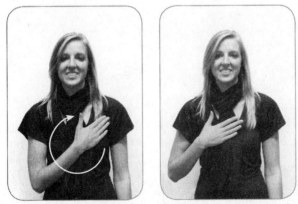

Place your hand over your heart, as demonstrated in the photo. Rotate in a clockwise fashion one or two times.

Purple:

Use the handshape for the letter "P." Rotate the wrist back and forth two times.

Push:

Imitate the motion of pushing someone or something.

- Q -

Quiet:

Imitate the normal quiet motion by placing one index finger in front of your mouth.

- R -

Rabbit:

Position your hands as demonstrated (cup the hands and place on sides of head, palms facing backward, to mimic bunny ears). Bend the fingers to show a bunny's ears flopping up and down. Repeat the motion two times.

Rain:

Place the handshape for the number 5 near the height of the forehead and move it downward at least twice to imitate the action of rain coming from the sky.

Rainbow:

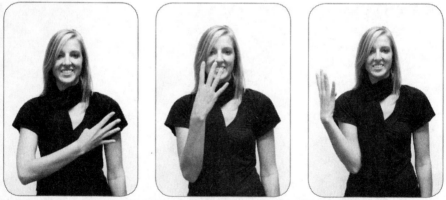

Make the handshape for the number 4 with the dominant hand, palm facing inward. Move the hand across your chest from left to right. Reverse the movement from right to left if the left hand is the dominant hand.

Read:

Position the fingers facing toward an open palm. Move up and down to demonstrate eyes moving along a page. The open fingers should be above the palm, not to the side.

Red:

With the index finger, move it from the top of your lip down one time. It is meant to reflect the color of your lips.

- S -

Sad:

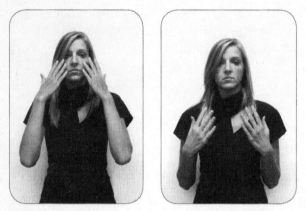

Pull the hands as demonstrated down, almost to resemble tears flowing down the face. However, do not touch the face.

See:

Using the handshape for the number 2, pull from near the eye out to resemble looking at something up close.

Share:

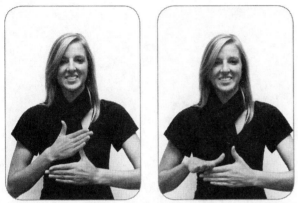

Position your hands as demonstrated. Move the dominant hand back and forth in the area depicted two times.

Shirt:

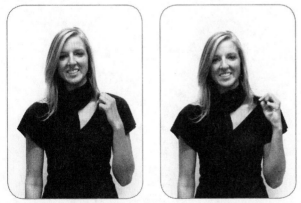

Pull at the corner of your shirt.

Shoes:

Make the handshape for the letter "S" with both hands. Position as demonstrated in the picture and bring together two times.

Sleep:

Start with an open curved hand near the eyes, as in the first photo, then bring down in a closing position. This is meant to demonstrate the act of "nodding off." You can also close your eyes for a brief second to truly show "sleeping."

Snow:

Use the handshape for the number 5. Start above your shoulder height and flutter the hands downward to simulate snowflakes moving through the air.

Socks:

Use your index fingers and alternate as shown in the photos.

Sorry:

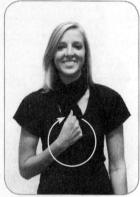

Using the handshape for the letter "A," place over your heart and rotate in a circle clockwise.

Stop:

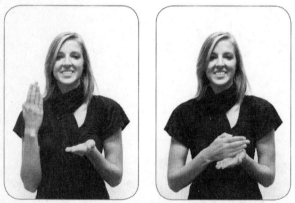

Position your non-dominant hand flat, palm facing upward. Position your dominant hand flat with the palm facing inward. Start with your hands in this position, as pictured on the left. Move the dominant hand and quickly place down on the open palm of the non-dominant hand.

Sun:

Make the handshape of the letter "C." Start at the side of your forehead and move out as depicted in the photos.

- T -

Telephone:

Imitate talking on a phone using the handshape "Y."

Thank You:

Start with the handshape as shown in the photo and pull away from the mouth.

Thirsty:

As depicted in the photos, place your finger to the side of your mouth and move it toward your upper chest one time.

Time:

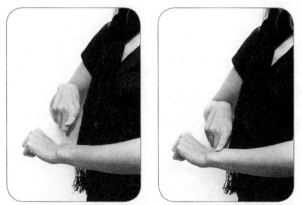

Point to where your watch would be on your wrist.

Tree:

Place your arms as shown in these photos. Wiggle your hand slightly to depict the motion of the top of a tree moving.

- W -

Wait:

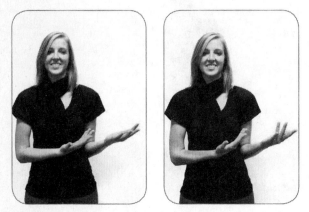

Place your arms and hands in front of your body, as demonstrated in the photos. Wiggle fingers two to three times.

Walk:

Place the hands in the position as in the photos. Alternate to mimic the act of walking.

Want:

Place your hands in front of you with the palms facing upward and fingers bent upward. Then pull your arm back to show bringing an object toward you.

Water:

Make the handshape for the letter "W," then tap your mouth twice with the index finger.

White:

Place the hand on your chest as depicted in the first photo. Pretend to pull your shirt, as demonstrated in the second photo. Pull away from your body.

- Y -

Yellow:

Use the handshape for the letter "Y." Rotate your wrist two times in front of your body, as depicted.

Yes:

Make a fist and move your wrist up and down. This imitates a head nodding "yes."

You're Welcome:

Position dominant hand in front of you with the palm facing upward. Bring your hand from the side to the front of your body.

Your/Yours:

Place the dominant hand in front of your chest with palm facing outward.

Appendix B

Information and Resources

Web sites to learn about sign language:

- **ASLInfo.com:** A great resource for parents to learn about sign language that can be used with hearing and deaf babies.

- **ASLpro.com:** A video dictionary of thousands of sign language words.

- **AslDeafined.com:** Sign language educational Web site.

- **Sign2me.com:** Provides resources for teaching your baby sign languages, as well as information about how to become a baby language sign instructor.

- **Kindersigns.com:** Provides various resources for teaching your baby sign languages, as well as information about how to become a baby language sign instructor.

- **BabySigns.com:** Provides many resources for teaching your baby sign languages, as well as information about how to become a baby language sign instructor.

- **Babystrology.com:** Includes a sign language dictionary.

- **Handspeak.com:** Handspeak offers offers an ASL online dictionary, ASL grammar, ASL storytelling and poetry, tips for fingerspelling, and more.

- **Aslcd.com:** Outlet to purchase supplemental resources, such as baby sign language DVDs.

- **Masterstech-home.com/ASLDICT.html:** A basic guide to learning ASL.

- **Deafresources.com:** Resources and technology for deaf and hard-of-hearing individuals.

- **Listen-up.org:** Resources for the deaf and hard of hearing.

- **Deafbiz.com:** Deaf resource center.

- **Deaf-culture-online.com:** Resounds and informationf or parents of deaf children.

- **Gallaudet.edu:** Gallaudet University's information for the hearing impaired.

Books on babies

- *The Baby Book*, by William Sears, M.D. and Martha Sears, R.N.

- *Attachment Parenting*, by Katie Allison Granju, William Sears, and Betsy Kennedy.

- *Your Baby and Child: From Birth to Age Five*, by Penelope Leach.

- *What to Expect the First Year*, by Heidi Murkoff, Sandee Hathawayand, B.S.N., Arlene Esenberg, and Sharon Mazel.

- *Secrets of the Baby Whisperer: How to Calm, Connect, and Communicate with Your Baby* by Tracy Hogg and Melinda Blau.

- *Baby's Eat, Sleep, & Poop Journal, Log Book* by Sandra Kosak.

- *Itsy Bitsy Yoga: Poses to Help Your Baby Sleep Longer, Digest Better, and Grow Stronger* by Helen Garabedian.

- *Baby Om: Yoga for Mothers and Babies* by Laura Staton and Sarah Perron.

- *Yogababy: Exercises to Help You Bond With Your Baby Physically, Emotionally and Spiritually* by DeAnsin Goodson Parker Ph.D. and Karen W. Bressler.

- *The Baby Owner's Manual: Operating Instructions, Trouble-Shooting Tips, and Advice on First-Year Maintenance* by Louis Borgenicht, Joe Borgenicht, Paul Kepple, and Jude Buffum.

- *The Postnatal Exercise Book: A Six Month Fitness Programme for Mother and Baby* by Barbara Whiteford and Margie Polde.

Books on baby/toddler sleep

- *The Baby Sleep Book: The Complete Guide to a Good Night's Rest for the Whole Family* by William Sears, M. D., Martha Sears, R. N., Robert W. Sears, M.D.

- *The 90-Minute Baby Sleep Program: Follow Your Child's Natural Sleep Rhythms for Better Nights and Naps* by Polly Moore.

- *The Happiest Baby on the Block: The New Way to Calm Crying and Help Your Newborn Baby Sleep Longer* by Harvey Karp.

- *On Becoming Baby Wise: Giving Your Infant the Gift of Nighttime Sleep* by Gary Ezzo and Robert Bucknam.

- *The Complete Idiot's Guide to Sleep Training your Child* by Ph.D., Melissa Burnham and Jennifer Lawler.

- *The No-Cry Sleep Solution for Toddlers and Preschoolers: Gentle Ways to Stop Bedtime Battles and Improve Your Childs Sleep* by Elizabeth Pantley.

- *Sleeping Through the Night, Revised Edition: How Infants, Toddlers, and Their Parents Can Get a Good Night's Sleep* by Jodi A. Mindell.

- *The Lull-A-Baby Sleep Plan: The Soothing, Superfast Way to Help Your New Baby Sleep Through the Night...and Prevent Sleep Problems Before They Develop* by Cathryn Tobin.

- *52 Sleep Secrets for Babies* by Kim West.

Bibliography

Beyer, Monica, *Baby Talk: A Guide to Using Basic Sign Language to Communicate with Your Baby*, Jeremy P. Tarcher/Penguin, New York, 2006.

Beyer, Monica, *Teach Your Baby To Sign: An Illustrated Guide To Simple Sign Language For Babies*, Fair Winds Press, Massachusetts, 2007.

Briant, Monta Z., *Baby Sign Language Basics: Early Communication for Hearing Babies and Toddlers*, Hay House, Inc., California, 2004.

Chambers, Diane P., *Communicating In Sign: Creative Ways to Learn Sign Language*, Simon & Schuster, New York, 1998.

Daniels, Marilyn, *Dancing With Words: Signing for Hearing Children's Literacy*, Bergin & Garvey, Connecticut, 2001.

Dennis, Kirsten & Azpiri, Tressa, *Sign To Learn: American Sign Language In The Early Childhood Classroom*, Redleaf press, Minnesota, 2005.

Fant, Lou, and Fant, Barbara, *The American Sign Language Phrase Book: Third Edition*, McGraw Hill Companies, New York, 2008.

Garcia, Dr. Joseph, *Sign With Your Baby: How To Communicate with Infants Before They Can Speak*, Northlight Communications, Inc., Washington, 2006.

Heller, Lora, *Sign Language For Kids*, Sterling Publishing Co., New York, 2004.

Lavelle, Yvonne K. and Kiddisign Training Company, *The Kiddisign Baby and Toddler Signing Course in American Sign Language, Second Edition*, Kiddisign Training Company, 2008.

Mindess, Anna, *Reading Between The Signs: Intercultural Communication for Sign Language Interpreters*, Second Edition Intercultural Press, Boston/London, 2006.

"Occupational Outlook Handbook, 2008-09 Edition," U.S. Department of Labor 2008-2009 handbook, **http://www.bls.gov/oco/ocos175.htm**.

Ryan, Diane, *The Complete Idiot's Guide to Baby Sign Language, Second Edition*, Penguin Group, New York, 2009.

Spencer, Patricia Ph.D., "A Good Start: Suggestions for Visual Conversations with Deaf and Hard-of-Hearing Babies and Toddlers," Gallaudet. edu, **http://clerccenter2.gallaudet.edu/KidsWorldDeafNEt/e-docs/visual-conversations/section-1.html**.

"What Are My Options?" Listen Up: The Basics, Listen-up.org, **www.listen-up.org/basics.htm**.

Author Biography

A writer, journalist, and editor for nearly two decades, Tracey Porpora is a successful freelance writer who has provided news, features, and analysis articles for dozens of consumer and trade magazines, Web sites, and major daily newspapers. She counts women's and parenting issues, health topics, and real estate issues among her favorite topics. When she is not writing, she enjoys spending time with her husband and their 5-year-old daughter, who loves learning new signs.

Index